FAITH CLINIC

VOLUME XX

- SHYNESS EDITION -

A place for the quiet, the cautious, and the spiritually willing who learned how to hide.

DR. PATRICIA S. TANNER

IBG Publications, Inc.

Published by I.B.G. Publications, Inc., a Power to Wealth Company

Web address: www.ibgpublications.com

admin@ibgpublications.com / 904-419-9810

Copyright, 2025 by Patricia S. Tanner

IBG Publications, Inc., Jacksonville, FL

ISBN: 978-1-971850-04-7

Tanner, Patricia S.

Faith Clinic, Volume XX- Shyness Edition- A Place For The Quiet, The Cautious And The Spiritually Willing

---

Printed in the United States of America.

DEDICATION

To the quiet ones who learned to shrink before they ever learned to speak.

To the thoughtful souls who feel deeply, think carefully, and love God fiercely, but often wonder if there is room for them in a world that rewards noise.

This book is dedicated to every person who was told they were "too quiet," too sensitive, too reserved and slowly began believing that presence required performance.

May you discover that you were never meant to become louder, only freer. May you find the courage to be seen without losing the beauty of who you are. And may you finally understand that your quiet was never the problem, fear was.

With compassion and conviction,

DR. PATRICIA S. TANNER

The Faith Doctor

DR. PATRICIA S. TANNER

TABLE OF CONTENTS

WELCOME TO THE FAITH CLINIC

You did not arrive here because something is wrong with you. You arrived here because somewhere along the way, being yourself started to feel unsafe. You learned how to manage your presence, measure your words, and quietly calculate how visible you were allowed to be in a room before it cost you peace. You learned how to smile politely, nod attentively, and keep the deeper parts of yourself tucked away where they could not be misunderstood, rejected, or put on the spot.

This clinic exists because too many people have confused shyness with deficiency. Too many believers have been taught, intentionally or not, that confidence is a spiritual requirement and that volume equals obedience. Somewhere between altar calls and icebreakers, between "step out in faith" and "don't be afraid," you were handed a message that said, *If you were braver, louder, quicker to speak, God could use you more.*

That message was never from Him.

The Faith Clinic is not here to push you into becoming someone louder, flashier, or more socially aggressive than you were designed to be. This is not a place where we medicate your personality or treat quietness like a disease. This is a place where we slow down enough to tell the truth: shyness is not a failure of faith, but hiding can quietly become one.

Here, we separate identity from coping mechanisms. We distinguish between being reserved and being afraid, between humility and self-erasure, between silence that is peaceful and silence that is protective. We are not here to rip away your boundaries or force you into uncomfortable exposure. We are here to ask gentle but necessary questions about why you feel safer unseen, why obedience feels optional when it requires visibility, and why being known sometimes feels more threatening than being faithful.

You do not need to rehearse answers here. You do not need to explain yourself or justify why you feel the way you do. You do not need to "warm up" before you belong. This clinic is designed for people who feel deeply, think carefully, and often carry more inside than they show on the outside.

So, take your time. Sit down. Let your shoulders drop. You are not late. You are not behind. You are not disappointing God by being quiet. But you are invited, gently, patiently, honestly, to stop disappearing from your own life.

Welcome to the Faith Clinic. You are not here to be fixed. You are here to be seen.

FAITH CLINIC PATIENT ID BRACELET

Shyness Edition: Identity Verification
(This page represents a spiritual ID band. You are not being labeled to limit you. You are being identified so you stop hiding.)

PATIENT NAME:

(Write your name as you are, not as you think you should be.)

ADMITTING FACILITY
Faith Clinic: Presence & Obedience Unit

PRIMARY DIAGNOSIS
Fear-Based Hiding Often misdiagnosed as humility, patience, or personality

SECONDARY SYMPTOMS
• Overthinking before speaking
• Delayed obedience labeled as wisdom
• Spiritual invisibility
• Self-erasure in the name of humility
• Avoidance disguised as peace

KNOWN TRIGGERS (ALLERGY ALERT)
☐ Being put on the spot
☐ Group discussions or public prayer
☐ Leadership visibility
☐ Misunderstanding or criticism
☐ Feeling "seen" without preparation

⚠ <u>WARNING:</u>

Extended exposure to avoidance may cause shrinking, stagnation, and loss of joy.

PRESCRIBED TREATMENT

Presence without performance Obedience without personality modification Courage without volume Visibility with boundaries

PATIENT RESTRICTIONS

- Do not require confidence before obedience
- Do not self-medicate with silence
- Do not confuse fear with discernment
- Do not wait for perfect timing
- Do not shrink to stay comfortable

EMERGENCY SCRIPTURE: READ IF FEAR SPIKES

- **2 Timothy 1:7** *God has not given me a spirit of fear, but of power, love, and a sound mind.*
- **James 1:22** *I am not just a listener. I am a doer.*
- **Matthew 5:14** *I am not designed to be hidden.*

PATIENT DECLARATION (READ DAILY)

I am not required to disappear to be faithful. I am not required to perform to be obedient. I am allowed to be present without being loud. I trust God with my visibility, my pace, and my personality. This is who I am, and I will not hide from my own life.

ATTENDING PHYSICIAN

The Holy Spirit *(Specialist in conviction, clarity, and courage without shame)*

<u>BRACELET NOTE</u>

This band does not come off when you feel better. It stays on while you heal. It stays on when fear whispers "later." It stays on when silence feels safer than obedience. You are tagged not for restriction, but for **remembrance**.

DR. PATRICIA S. TANNER

INTRODUCTION

At some point in your life, you realize that being noticeable came with consequences. Maybe it was being misunderstood when you finally spoke up. Maybe it was being overlooked so often that speaking felt pointless. Maybe it was a moment when all eyes turned toward you and your body reacted before your faith could catch up, heart racing, throat tight, mind blank.

Whatever the moment was, something in you decided that visibility was risky, and retreat felt safer. So, you adapted. You learned how to blend in without fully disappearing. You learned how to participate just enough to avoid attention, how to serve quietly without being seen, and how to love God deeply without letting anyone else know how much it cost you. You learned how to call wisdom, maturity, or discernment. But beneath those labels there was often a quieter truth: fear had learned how to sound spiritual.

This book exists because shyness, when left unexamined, does not stay neutral. Over time, it can turn into avoidance. Avoidance can turn into hiding. And hiding, even when it feels peaceful, slowly shrinks the space you believe you are allowed to occupy. You begin to edit your prayers, your gifts, your questions, and eventually your obedience, not because God asked you to, but because fear convinced you it was safer.

This Is Me is not a demand to become bold overnight or a challenge to suddenly love attention. It is an invitation to stop confusing your personality with your protection strategies. It is a slow, honest examination of the moments when you choose comfort over calling, silence over truth, and invisibility overgrowth, not out of rebellion, but out of exhaustion.

This book is for the person who feels God's pull but hesitates at the cost. For the one who knows they are called but hopes calling will never require a microphone, a conversation, or a visible step forward. It is for the believer who keeps telling themselves that staying quiet is the same as staying faithful, while secretly wondering why life feels so small.

God never asked you to become louder to be worthy. He asked you to become honest enough to stop hiding. He is not offended by your shyness, but He is deeply invested in your freedom. Freedom from the need to disappear. Freedom from the belief that being seen automatically leads to rejection. Freedom to say, without flinching or apologizing, *This is who I am, and I trust God here too.*

This book will not rush you. It will not shame you. It will not force you into performative confidence. Instead, it will walk with you as you learn the difference between who you are and who fear taught you to be. It will help you recognize where you have been shrinking out of habit rather than conviction, and where God has been patiently waiting, not for a louder version of you, but for a truer one.

This is not a declaration of arrival. It is a declaration of presence. This is not bravado. It is honesty. This is not you becoming someone else. This is you finally being able to say, without shrinking back: *This is me.*

📋 FAITH CLINIC INTAKE FORM

Shyness Edition

Patient   Name: ___________________________

(You can write your name here—or leave it blank if even that feels like too much today.)

Reason for Visit:

I am not broken, but I am tired of disappearing. I want to understand why staying quiet feels safer than being known, even when I love God deeply and desire to live fully. I am here because I sense that my shyness may no longer be neutral, it may be quietly shaping my obedience, my relationships, and my sense of self.

Primary Symptoms (check all that apply):

☐ Avoiding attention even when you feel prompted to speak or act

☐ Rehearsing conversations in your head but rarely having them

☐ Feeling spiritually willing but socially paralyzed

☐ Sitting in the background to avoid being noticed

☐ Confusing peace with avoidance

☐ Shrinking your personality to make others comfortable

☐ Feeling unseen but also afraid of being seen

☐ Saying "that's just how I am" while secretly wanting more

Duration of Symptoms:

- Longer than I would like to admit. Possibly years. Possibly since childhood. Possibly since the last time being visible hurt more than it healed.

Previous Treatments Attempted:

Trying to "just be bold." Praying harder without addressing fear. Waiting for confidence to magically arrive. Calling silence wisdom. Avoiding situations that require presence.

Patient Statement (optional):
(This is where you can finally say what you usually swallow.)

Clinician's Note:
Patient presents as thoughtful, sincere, spiritually aware, and emotionally guarded. No signs of rebellion. Strong indicators of fear-based self-protection masked as humility. Prognosis is hopeful with gentle honesty, consistent presence, and grace-based courage.

FAITH CLINIC: EMERGENCY WALLET CARD

For Moments When Fear Tries to Take Control
(Keep this card with you. Read it when your chest tightens, your mind races, or silence feels safer than obedience.)

PATIENT STATUS

Currently under treatment for **Fear-Based Hiding** *(This is not a failure. This is awareness.)*

PRIMARY SYMPTOM ALERT

If you are feeling the urge to:
• Stay quiet when you know you should speak
• Delay obedience and call it "later"
• Shrink your presence to stay comfortable
• Overthink until the moment passes
• Disappear and call it humility
STOP. PAUSE. READ THIS CARD.

EMERGENCY REMINDER

Fear feels urgent.
Obedience does not rush.
Presence does not require perfection.
You do not need confidence to act.
You do not need permission to exist.
You do not need to disappear to be faithful.

IMMEDIATE INSTRUCTIONS

1. Take one slow breath.
2. Place both feet on the ground.
3. Ask yourself one honest question:
"Am I hiding, or am I trusting?"
Then choose one small act of presence. Not everything. Just one.

TRUTH TO OVERRIDE PANIC

God has not asked you to be loud.
God has asked you to be available.
Fear is familiar, but it is not in charge.

EMERGENCY SCRIPTURE

- ✓ **2 Timothy 1:7** *God has not given me a spirit of fear, but of power, love, and a sound mind.*
- ✓ **James 1:22** *I am not just a listener. I am a doer.*
- ✓ **Psalm 27:8** *My heart says, "Seek His face." I will seek Him here, not hide.*

PATIENT DECLARATION

I choose presence over protection.
I choose obedience over delay.
I choose honesty over hiding.
I am safe to be seen.
God is with me here.

IF SYMPTOMS PERSIST

Remain present.
Do not retreat.
Fear will lower its voice when it is not obeyed.

ATTENDING PHYSICIAN

The Holy Spirit
On call always
Specialist in clarity, courage, and calm

BACK OF CARD: QUIET REMINDER

You are not behind.
You are not broken.
You are not failing.
You are healing in real time.
This is you choosing not to hide.

PERSONAL NOTES

Part 1:

SYMPTOMS

What shyness looks like when it's running the show.

PERSONAL NOTES

Chapter 1

When Quiet Turns Into Hiding

SYMPTOM

"I'm just not the kind of person who speaks up."

This symptom rarely presents itself as a problem at first. In fact, it often feels like a reasonable and even admirable personality trait. Many people who experience it describe themselves as thoughtful, reflective, introverted, or simply not interested in drawing attention to themselves. They believe they are mature, considerate, and self-aware. They may even feel spiritually affirmed in their quietness, especially if they have been praised for being humble, easygoing, or low maintenance. Because of this, the symptom is often overlooked, minimized, or misunderstood, both by the individual experiencing it and by those around them.

Over time, however, what began as a natural preference for quiet starts to influence behavior in more limiting ways. Situations that require visibility begin to feel increasingly uncomfortable. Speaking up, sharing an opinion, volunteering, praying aloud, or stepping into leadership roles triggers anxiety rather than anticipation. The individual may feel a strong internal sense of agreement or calling yet find themselves hesitating or withdrawing when action is required. This hesitation is not rooted in a lack of conviction, but in a growing discomfort with being seen, heard, or evaluated by others.

As the symptom progresses, the internal world becomes increasingly active while the external world becomes more restricted. Thoughts are rehearsed repeatedly before conversations that never happen. Words are weighed, edited, and often discarded before they are ever spoken. After social or spiritual interactions, moments are replayed mentally, searching for perceived mistakes or missed cues. This constant internal monitoring creates emotional fatigue, which reinforces the belief that silence is safer and less costly than participation. Gradually, silence stops being a choice and becomes a default response.

Avoidance begins to take shape in subtle ways. The individual may gravitate toward roles that allow them to remain behind the scenes, even when they sense a desire to contribute more directly. They may choose seating that minimizes attention, avoid eye contact when questions are asked, or deter opportunities by convincing themselves that someone else is more qualified or better suited. These decisions are rarely framed as fear. Instead, they are explained as practicality, humility, or patience. Yet beneath those explanations is often a deep concern about being misunderstood, rejected, or exposed.

One of the most confusing aspects of this symptom is the emotional contradiction it produces. The individual may feel unseen, overlooked, or underutilized, while simultaneously working to remain unnoticed. There is a desire for connection 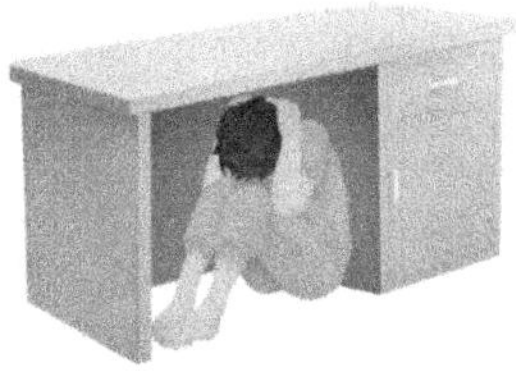 and purpose, paired with a strong instinct to withdraw when those things require vulnerability. This tension creates a persistent sense of dissatisfaction that is difficult to articulate. The person may love God sincerely and remain faithful in private practices yet feel stalled or unfulfilled in their spiritual life.

Spiritual rationalization frequently accompanies this symptom. Silence is reframed as humility, avoidance as discernment, and delay as wisdom. The individual reassures themselves that God understands their heart and that obedience can wait until circumstances feel safer or more comfortable. Over time, fear adapts to spiritual language and becomes difficult to identify. Rather than rejecting faith, the individual learns how to practice it within carefully controlled boundaries that minimize emotional risk.

This pattern often has roots in earlier experiences where visibility led to discomfort or harm. Being misunderstood, dismissed, criticized, or embarrassed can teach a person that it is safer to remain quiet and unassuming. These lessons do not disappear with time; they evolve. As the individual matures, fear learns how to coexist with faith, allowing belief to remain intact while subtly shaping behavior. Obedience becomes selective, guided not by rebellion, but by self-protection.

Physically, this symptom may present as tension, shallow breathing, racing thoughts, or mental blankness when required to speak or step forward. These bodily responses reinforce the belief that visibility is dangerous, even when there is no actual threat present. Over time, this reinforces avoidance and contributes to feelings of frustration and self-criticism. The individual may wonder why their faith feels strong internally, yet it is so difficult to express outwardly.

Eventually, hiding becomes familiar and socially acceptable. The individual may be described as reliable, kind, or faithful, yet rarely seen in positions that require initiative or leadership. While others may not recognize the struggle, the individual often carries a quiet grief related to unrealized potential. They sense that they are living below their capacity, but the thought of stepping forward continues to feel overwhelming. This is the point at which quiet has fully transitioned into hiding, not as an act of rebellion, but as a learned way of surviving.

TEACHING

Quiet Is Not the Enemy, Fear Is

Scripture consistently affirms that quietness itself is not a flaw or failure. Many biblical figures wrestled with hesitation, insecurity, and fear long before they ever stepped into their calling. Moses doubted his ability to speak. Jeremiah questioned his readiness and

credibility. Gideon struggled with feelings of inadequacy. Esther remained silent for a season before speaking at great personal risk. Even Jesus chose silence at critical moments rather than defending Himself or performing for approval. These examples demonstrate that God does not require a loud personality to accomplish His purposes.

The problem arises when fear begins to define the limits of obedience. Fear rarely presents itself in obvious or dramatic ways. Instead, it speaks in measured, logical tones. It encourages caution, delay, and restraint. It suggests that waiting is wise and that avoiding exposure is prudent. Over time, fear begins to shape decision-making, not by opposing faith directly, but by quietly setting boundaries around it. The individual continues to believe, serve, and pray, but only within areas that feel emotionally safe.

Faith, according to Scripture, is inherently active. James teaches that faith without work is dead, emphasizing that belief is meant to move and express itself through obedience. This does not imply that God demands performance or extroversion. Rather, it highlights that faith is designed to respond. When quiet turns into hiding, obedience becomes conditional, practiced only when it aligns with comfort. Delay is reframed as discernment, and fear is mistaken for wisdom. Matthew's declaration that believers are the light of the world speaks to identity rather than personality. Light, by its nature, is visible. This does not mean that every believer must be outspoken or publicly expressive, but it does mean that faith is not meant to be concealed indefinitely. When individuals consistently hide to feel safe, they are not protecting humility; they are restricting the expression of what God has already placed within them.

God does not require confidence as a prerequisite for obedience. Throughout Scripture, action often precedes assurance. The Israelites stepped forward before the sea parted. Peter left the boat before he knew whether he could walk on water. These moments illustrate that trust is demonstrated through movement, not emotional readiness. Waiting to feel confident before obeying often results in stagnation rather than growth.

God's patience with fear does not mean He endorses it. He understands hesitation, but He continually invites people beyond it. He distinguishes between personality and protection, between temperament and fear-based limitation. When individuals allow fear to dictate the terms of their obedience, life becomes increasingly constrained. Opportunities diminish, relationships remain surface-level, and spiritual growth feels stalled, not because God withholds, but because fear restricts access.

Healing begins with honest recognition. Not dramatic declarations or forced boldness, but a willingness to acknowledge where fear has  quietly assumed authority. God does not call individuals to abandon who they are; He calls them to trust Him with who they are. Quiet is not the enemy. Fear is. And when fear is no longer allowed to decide what obedience looks like, presence begins to replace hiding, and growth becomes possible again.

♂ FAITH PRESCRIPTION

Presence Before Confidence

Dosage: Daily, especially when uncomfortable
Instructions: Do not wait to feel ready before acting. Your prescription is not to "be bold." Your prescription is to ***be present***. Confidence is not a prerequisite for obedience; it is often the result of it. Waiting to feel confident before obeying is like waiting to feel strong before you ever lift a weight.

Start small. Speak one sentence instead of none. Stay in the room five minutes longer than you want to. Say yes to the assignment even if your voice shakes. These are not insignificant acts; they are spiritual exposure therapy. Fear loses authority when it is challenged gently but consistently.

SPIRITUAL VITAMIN

Vitamin P: Presence

Scripture: Psalm 27:8 says, *"My heart says of you, 'Seek His face!' Your face, Lord, I will seek."*

Presence is discipline. You practice it before you master it. This vitamin strengthens your spiritual muscles by reminding you that God's face, not people's reactions, is the place you belong. Take this vitamin daily by asking, *"Where am I tempted to hide today?"* and choosing one small act of presence instead.

HOLY SPIRIT CONSULT

Holy Spirit, where have I been confusing my personality with my fear? Where have I been calling avoidance wisdom? Where are You inviting me to show up, not loudly, but honestly? Listen without rushing. Conviction may feel uncomfortable, but it is never cruel.

GUIDED PRAYER

"God, I confess that I have learned how to hide in ways that feel spiritual. I have chosen silence when You were inviting obedience. I have shrunk myself to feel safe, even when You were calling me forward.

I thank You that You are not angry with me, but patient. Teach me the difference between who I am and who fear taught me to be. Give me the courage to be present, even when I don't feel confident. I trust You with my visibility. Amen."

📝 JOURNAL REFLECTION PAGE

- Where do I most often choose silence over obedience?

____

____

____

- What am I afraid will happen if I am seen?

____

____

____

- What is one small act of presence God may be inviting me into this week?

____

____

____

- How would my life look different if fear stopped editing my faith?

____

____

____

____

Chapter 2

Overthinking Every Word Before You Say It (And Still Saying Nothing)

SYMPTOM

"I just like to think things through before I speak."

This symptom often presents itself as intelligence, self-awareness, or emotional maturity. People who experience it frequently describe themselves as thoughtful communicators who value precision and clarity. They do not want to say the wrong thing, offend someone, misrepresent their intentions, or appear foolish. At face value, this sounds responsible. It often becomes a quiet prison where every thought must pass through multiple layers of internal approval before it is allowed into the world.

Overthinking does not begin as paralysis. It begins as caution. The  individual considers different outcomes, weighs possible reactions, and anticipates how their words might be received. However, as this habit deepens, thinking replaces acting. Conversations are rehearsed internally long before they ever occur, and many of them never do. The mind becomes a staging area for dialogue that rarely leaves the rehearsal phase. By the time an opportunity to speak arrives, the individual is already exhausted by the internal process.

This symptom is marked by constant mental editing. Words are revised before they are spoken. Tone is analyzed before it is used. Timing is scrutinized until the moment passes. The individual may feel fully engaged internally while remaining externally silent. This creates a disconnect between what they know and what they express. Over time, this gap grows wider, leading to frustration and self-doubt. The individual begins questioning why they struggle to communicate something they understand so clearly in their own mind.

Fear plays a significant role in sustaining this symptom, even when it is not acknowledged. The fear may not be dramatic, but it is persistent. It includes fear of being misunderstood, fear of being judged, fear of saying something incorrect, and fear of drawing attention. These fears are rarely named directly. Instead, they are disguised as a desire to be accurate, respectful, or spiritually careful. The individual convinces themselves that silence is preferable to the risk of imperfection.

As overthinking becomes habitual, opportunities for expression steadily decline. The individual may hesitate to ask questions, offer insights, or share personal experiences. They may avoid conversations that feel unpredictable or emotionally charged. Even when prompted, they may default to short or neutral responses to avoid revealing too much. Over time, others may assume they have little to contribute, reinforcing the individual's belief that staying quiet is the safer option.

This symptom also impacts spiritual life. Prayers become carefully worded rather than honest. Worship becomes internal rather than expressive. Testimonies remain unshared, not because they lack power, but because articulating them feels overwhelming. The individual may deeply believe God's truth while struggling to speak it aloud, especially in communal settings. This creates a sense of isolation, where faith feels deeply personal but difficult to communicate.

Physically, overthinking can manifest mental fatigue, tension, and difficulty focusing on conversations. The individual may feel mentally "ahead" of the present moment, analyzing possibilities rather than engaging with what is happening. This constant cognitive activity leaves little room for spontaneity or genuine connection. The individual may leave interactions feeling dissatisfied, replaying what they wished they had said rather than what they experienced.

Eventually, overthinking leads to inaction. The individual may recognize that they have valuable insight but still feel unable to share it. They may grow frustrated with themselves, interpreting their silence as a personal failure rather than a learned response. This reinforces shame and avoidance, strengthening the cycle. The symptom persists not because the individual lacks courage or conviction, but because fear has trained the mind to prioritize safety over expression.

TEACHING

Thinking Is Not Discernment When It Replaces Obedience

Scripture affirms wisdom, reflection, and self-control, but it never elevates endless analysis above obedience. Discernment is meant to clarify action, not delay it indefinitely. When overthinking dominates decision-making, it often masquerades as spiritual maturity while quietly undermining trust. The individual may believe they are being careful when they are avoiding the vulnerability required to act.

Biblical faith consistently emphasizes responsiveness over certainty. Many figures in Scripture acted with limited information and imperfect understanding. Abraham left familiar territory without knowing the destination. Peter stepped out of the boat without guarantees. The disciples followed Jesus before fully comprehending His mission. These examples highlight that faith is not dependent on complete mental clarity, but on willingness to respond when called.

Overthinking creates the illusion of control. By mentally rehearsing outcomes, the individual feels temporarily protected from uncertainty. However, this protection is false. Life remains unpredictable regardless of preparation, and obedience often requires movement before reassurance. When thinking replaces trusting, the individual may feel spiritually stagnant despite genuine belief. Growth is delayed not because God is silent, but because fear has become the filter through which decisions are made.

Scripture repeatedly warns against leaning exclusively on one's own understanding. This does not mean abandoning thought or reason but recognizing their limits. Overthinking often signals an attempt to manage outcomes rather than trust God with them. When the mind is consumed with hypothetical reactions, it becomes difficult to remain present and attentive to the moment where obedience is required.

Spiritually, overthinking can distance the individual from God's voice. The constant internal dialogue leaves little space for listening. Instead of responding to prompt, the individual debates it. Instead of stepping forward, they seek reassurance through analysis. Over time, this pattern dulls spiritual sensitivity, not because God stops speaking, but because the mind is too occupied to respond.

God does not ask for perfect words. He asks for availability. Throughout Scripture, God works through people who speak imperfectly, act hesitantly, and move forward despite uncertainty. Overthinking delays obedience by demanding emotional and intellectual comfort before action. Faith, however, is often expressed through imperfect steps taken in trust.

Healing begins when the individual recognizes that overthinking is not a sign of depth, but a signal of fear-driven self-protection. This recognition is not meant to shame, but to invite honesty. God is not frustrated by thoughtful people, but He does invite them to trust Him beyond their own mental safeguards. When thinking is surrendered to faith rather than used to control outcomes, obedience becomes possible again.

🖊 FAITH PRESCRIPTION

Stop Rehearsing. Start Responding.

The prescribed treatment for overthinking is not intellectual discipline, but relational trust. Overthinking thrives when the mind believes it must manage outcomes to stay safe. Faith, however, grows when responsibility for outcomes is surrendered to God rather than controlled internally. The goal of this prescription is not to silence thought, but to interrupt the cycle where thinking replaces responding.

The patient is instructed to practice responding before rehearsing. This means allowing words to be spoken before they are perfected, questions to be asked before they are fully refined, and actions to be taken before emotional certainty arrives. This practice will feel uncomfortable at first, especially for those who have relied on mental preparation as a form of protection. Discomfort should not be interpreted as danger, but as evidence that fear is being challenged.

This prescription requires consistency rather than intensity. The patient is encouraged to speak once when they normally remain silent, to answer honestly rather than strategically, and to allow imperfection without self-punishment. Over time, the mind will learn that safety does not come from flawless expression, but from trusting God to meet you in real-time obedience.

🧬 SPIRITUAL VITAMIN

Vitamin T: Trust
Scripture Reference: Proverbs 3:5–6

This vitamin supports the gradual weakening of fear-based thinking by strengthening trust in God's guidance rather than personal analysis. The patient is encouraged to take this vitamin daily by intentionally releasing the need to predict outcomes. Trust grows not when everything is understood, but when obedience is practiced despite uncertainty.

The patient may experience withdrawal symptoms such as anxiety, hesitation, or the urge to retreat into overthinking. These symptoms are temporary and indicate that the old coping mechanism is losing dominance. Continued intake will result in increased clarity, reduced mental fatigue, and greater confidence rooted in experience rather than imagination.

HOLY SPIRIT CONSULT

Holy Spirit, show me where I have mistaken overthinking for wisdom. Reveal the moments when I have delayed obedience because I wanted to feel more prepared rather than more trusting. Help me recognize when my mind is trying to protect me from discomfort instead of leading me toward growth. Teach me how to listen without debating and how to respond without rehearsing.

The patient is encouraged to sit with these questions without rushing to answer them. Insight often comes through awareness rather than analysis.

GUIDED PRAYER

"God, I acknowledge that I have relied on my thoughts to keep me safe. I believed that if I could think far enough ahead, I could avoid embarrassment, rejection, or failure. I recognize now that this habit has kept me silent when You were inviting me to speak and hesitant when You were calling me to act. I ask You to help me trust You more than my own understanding. Teach me to respond when Your

prompt me, even if my words are imperfect and my confidence is incomplete. I place my thoughts under Your authority and choose obedience over analysis. Amen."

📝 JOURNAL REFLECTION PAGE

- Where do I most often rehearse conversations instead of having them, and what am I afraid might happen if I spoke honestly in those moments?

____

____

____

____

____

____

- How has overthinking helped me feel safe in the past, and how might it now be limiting my growth?

____

____

____

____

____

____

____

- What is one recent moment when I sensed a prompting to speak or act but hesitated, and what thoughts held me back?

- What would trusting God in real time look like for me this week, even if it feels uncomfortable?

PERSONAL NOTES

Chapter 3
Loving God Deeply, But Staying Invisible

SYMPTOM

"I don't need to be seen. God knows my heart."

This symptom often develops quietly and is rarely confronted because it appears spiritually sound on the surface. The individual genuinely loves God, values faith, and desires to live in alignment with His will. They pray privately, read Scripture, and maintain an internal devotion that feels sincere and meaningful. Because of this, the decision to remain unseen does not initially feel problematic. It feels reverent, humble, and safe. The belief that God knows the heart becomes a comforting justification for staying hidden.

Over time, however, this mindset begins to shape behavior in subtle but significant ways. The individual avoids opportunities that require visible faith, such as sharing testimonies, serving in leadership, or expressing belief openly. They may decline roles that place them in front of others, not because they lack conviction, but because visibility feels unnecessary or uncomfortable. The idea that faith can remain private becomes increasingly appealing, especially when public expression feels risky or draining.

As this pattern continues, spiritual invisibility becomes normalized. The individual convinces themselves that impact does not require presence and that obedience can remain internal. They may admire bold faith in others while quietly exempting themselves from similar expectations. Over time, they begin to believe that being unseen protects their relationship with God from scrutiny, misunderstanding, or pressure.

This symptom is often reinforced by past experiences where visibility resulted in discomfort or harm. Being judged, misunderstood, or spiritually pressured can lead an individual to associate public faith with emotional risk. To avoid repeating those experiences, they retreat into private devotion, believing that intimacy with God does not require outward expression. While private devotion is valuable, it becomes limited when it replaces visible obedience.

Emotionally, this symptom creates a quiet disconnect. The individual may feel spiritually alive but relationally distant. They may long for deeper connection within the faith community while resisting the vulnerability required to build it. Over time, faith becomes increasingly internalized, making it difficult for others to truly know or support them. This isolation often goes unnoticed because the individual appears faithful and consistent.

Spiritually, invisibility can lead to stagnation. Growth slows when faith is never tested publicly. Opportunities for encouragement, accountability, and shared experience are missed. The individual may feel called to more yet remain hesitant to step into roles that require visibility. This creates a persistent tension between devotion and hesitation, where love for God exists alongside fear of being seen.

TEACHING

Private Faith Was Never Meant To Replace Visible Obedience

Scripture consistently affirms the value of private devotion, but it never presents invisibility as the goal of faith. Jesus taught about praying in secret and avoiding performative spirituality, yet He also called His followers to be witnesses, ambassadors, and examples. Faith was always intended to be both internal and external, personal and communal. When faith becomes entirely private, it loses one of its essential expressions.

The idea that God knowing the heart is sufficient can become misleading when it is used to avoid visible obedience. God does know the heart, but He also shapes it through action. Throughout Scripture, obedience is often public, not for recognition, but for transformation. Abraham's faith was demonstrated through action. Esther's faith required visibility. The early church's faith was expressed through shared life and public witness.

When individuals remain invisible, they may protect themselves from criticism, but they also limit their influence. Faith that is never expressed outwardly cannot encourage others, challenge injustice, or build community. God's design for faith includes relationship, accountability, and shared testimony. Invisibility restricts these elements, not because God demands performance, but because growth often occurs through participation.

Jesus described believers as light and salt, metaphors that imply presence and impact. Light that is hidden cannot illuminate. Salt that remains unused cannot be preserved. These metaphors emphasize that faith, by its nature, is meant to interact with the world. Remaining unseen may feel safe, but it ultimately contradicts the relational nature of the gospel.

Visible obedience does not require constant exposure or performative faith. It requires availability. It involves responding when God prompts, even if it feels uncomfortable. God does not ask individuals to abandon their temperament, but He does invite them to trust Him with their visibility. Faith grows when individuals allow themselves to be seen, not for approval, but for alignment with God's purposes.

FAITH PRESCRIPTION

Practice Visible Faith Without Performing

The prescribed treatment for spiritual invisibility is intentional visibility rooted in obedience rather than attention-seeking. The patient is encouraged to engage in acts of faith that are seen by others, not to gain recognition, but to resist the habit of hiding. This may involve sharing a testimony, participating in group prayer, or accepting roles that require presence.

The patient should focus on obedience rather than outcome. Visible faith does not require flawless execution or emotional confidence. It requires willingness. By practicing presence in small, consistent ways, the individual learns that being seen does not automatically result in harm. Over time, fear loses its influence, and faith becomes more integrated into daily life.

☤ SPIRITUAL VITAMIN

Vitamin V: Visibility
Scripture Reference: Matthew 5:16

This vitamin supports the integration of internal belief with external expression. The patient is encouraged to take this vitamin by allowing faith to be seen in everyday actions. Visibility is not about self-promotion, but about alignment. Continued intake strengthens confidence rooted in obedience rather than approval.

🕊 HOLY SPIRIT CONSULT

Holy Spirit reveals where I have hidden my faith out of fear rather than conviction. Show me the opportunities I have avoided because visibility felt uncomfortable. Teach me how to trust You with being seen, even when it feels vulnerable. Help me practice obedience that reflects my love for You openly and honestly. The patient is encouraged to listen to conviction rather than condemnation during this consultation.

🙏 GUIDED PRAYER

"God, I thank You that You know my heart completely. I also recognize that You call me to live my faith openly, not to impress others, but to reflect You. I confess that I have chosen invisibility when obedience required presence.

Help me trust You with my visibility. Teach me how to live my faith honestly, without hiding or performing. I place my fear in Your hands and choose obedience even when it feels uncomfortable. Amen."

📝 JOURNAL REFLECTION PAGE

- In what ways have I kept my faith private to avoid discomfort or exposure?

____

____

____

____

____

- What opportunities for visible obedience have I declined, and what fears influenced those decisions?

____

____

____

____

____

- How might my faith grow if I allowed others to see it more openly?

____

____

____

____

____

____

____

- What is one small way I can practice visible faith this week without performing?

____

____

____

____

____

____

____

____

____

____

____

PERSONAL NOTES

Chapter 4

"I'll Speak Up Later" And Other Lies Fear Tells You

How procrastinated obedience disguises itself as patience

SYMPTOM

"I just need more time before I step into that."

This symptom is especially difficult to identify because it sounds wise, mature, and spiritually responsible. The individual experiencing it often believes they are being patient, thoughtful, and respectful of timing. They are not refusing obedience outright. Instead, they are postponing it. The phrase "later" becomes a placeholder that feels harmless but gradually turns into a pattern. Over time, obedience is not denied but endlessly deferred.

People who struggle with this symptom often feel a genuine internal pull toward certain actions, conversations, or responsibilities. They sense God's prompting, recognize opportunities to step forward, and even feel excitement about what could be. However, when the moment arrives, hesitation sets in. The individual convinces themselves that they need more preparation, more clarity, more confidence, or better circumstances before acting. Delays feel safer than risk and waiting feels easier than stepping forward while uncertain.

As this pattern continues, "later" becomes increasingly vague. What was once a short pause turns into weeks, months, or even years of postponement. The individual may still talk about what they plan to do eventually, but action never quite arrives. They may revisit the idea repeatedly in their mind, reassuring themselves that timing will eventually align. Meanwhile, opportunities quietly pass, and the sense of urgency fades.

This symptom often carries an emotional weight that is difficult to articulate. The individual may feel frustrated with themselves for not acting, yet also relieved that they have avoided immediate discomfort. This internal conflict creates a cycle where guilt and relief coexist. The person knows they are capable of more, but fear continues to set the pace. Over time, delayed obedience becomes normalized, and inaction feels justified rather than concerned.

Spiritually, this symptom can feel confusing because it exists alongside sincere devotion. The individual prays, reflects, and seeks God, believing that patience is a virtue. They may reference wisdom, discernment, or waiting on the Lord as reasons for delay. However, beneath these explanations is often a quiet fear of exposure, failure, or responsibility. Fear does not say no; it says not yet, creating the illusion of faithfulness while avoiding commitment.

As procrastinated obedience becomes habitual, confidence erodes. Each delayed opportunity reinforces the belief that stepping forward is difficult or dangerous. The individual may begin to doubt their own ability to act decisively, interpreting hesitation as a personal flaw rather than a learned response. Over time, the habit of waiting for shape's identity, and the individual begins to see themselves as someone who thinks deeply but struggles to act.

TEACHING

Waiting On God Is Not The Same As Avoiding Obedience

Scripture affirms the value of patience, but it does not support indefinite delay when obedience is clear. Waiting on God is an active posture of trust, not a passive avoidance of responsibility. Throughout Scripture, waiting is often paired with preparation and movement rather than stagnation. When fear disguises itself as patience, waiting becomes disconnected from obedience and rooted instead in self-protection.

God's guidance is not always accompanied by complete clarity or comfort. Many biblical figures acted with limited information and significant uncertainty. Noah built before rain was visible. Abraham left before knowing the destination. Esther spoke before knowing the outcome. These examples illustrate that obedience often precedes reassurance. Delaying action until fear subsides is not faith; it is an attempt to control the emotional cost of obedience.

Fear thrives in delay because delay reduces immediate discomfort. Each postponed step provides temporary relief, reinforcing the habit. However, this relief is short-lived and often followed by regret or self-doubt.

Over time, delay shapes perception, making obedience feel increasingly intimidating. What once felt manageable begins to feel overwhelming, not because the task changed, but because fear was allowed to grow unchecked.

Jesus frequently called people to immediate response. His invitations were often simple and direct, requiring movement rather than prolonged contemplation. While discernment is necessary in complex situations, many instances of procrastinated obedience stem not from uncertainty, but from fear of being seen, misunderstood, or stretched. When obedience is delayed for emotional comfort, it loses its formative power.

Waiting becomes unhealthy when it replaces trust with control. Instead of trusting God with the outcome, the individual attempts to manage risk by postponing action. This approach limits growth and keeps faith theoretically rather than lived. God's timing is not an excuse for avoidance; it is an invitation to trust Him while moving forward.

Healing begins when the individual learns to distinguish between true waiting and fear-based delay. True waiting keeps the heart open and responsive. Fear-based delay narrows the heart and reinforces avoidance. When obedience is practiced promptly and imperfectly, fear loses its influence, and trust grows through experience rather than anticipation.

💊 FAITH PRESCRIPTION

Respond Promptly, Even When You Feel Unready

The prescribed treatment for procrastinated obedience is intentional responsiveness. The patient is encouraged to act when clarity is sufficient, rather than waiting for emotional readiness. This does not mean acting impulsively, but it does mean recognizing when delay is no longer serving wisdom but reinforcing fear.

The patient should practice responding within a reasonable timeframe when prompted, even if discomfort remains. Over time, this practice retrains the nervous system and builds confidence rooted in obedience rather than certainty. Prompt response reduces the power of fear and strengthens trust through lived experience.

🧬 SPIRITUAL VITAMIN

Vitamin R: Responsiveness
Scripture Reference: James 1:22

This vitamin supports the transition from intention to action. The patient is encouraged to take this vitamin daily by noticing moments of delay and choosing timely obedience instead. Consistent intake results in increased spiritual momentum and reduced hesitation.

🕊 HOLY SPIRIT CONSULT

Holy Spirit shows me where I have been delaying obedience under the label of patience. Reveal the opportunities I have postponed out of fear rather than wisdom. Teach me how to trust You enough to respond promptly when You lead me forward.

Help me recognize when waiting is faithful and when it is simply avoidance. The patient is encouraged to remain open to conviction without defensiveness.

🙏 GUIDED PRAYER

"God, I acknowledge that I have postponed obedience because waiting felt safer than acting. I confess that I have used patience as a shield against discomfort and responsibility.

Teach me how to trust You with timely obedience, even when I feel unprepared. Give me the courage to respond when You prompt me, and the wisdom to recognize when delay is rooted in fear rather than faith. I choose responsiveness over avoidance and trust You with the outcome. Amen."

📝 JOURNAL REFLECTION PAGE

- Where in my life have I been saying "later" instead of responding in obedience?

____

____

____

____

- What fears surface when I consider acting sooner rather than waiting?

____

____

____

____

- How has delaying action affected my confidence and spiritual growth?

- What is one specific step I sense God inviting me to take now rather than later?

PERSONAL NOTES

Part 2:

THE DIAGNOSIS
What's really happening beneath the silence

PERSONAL NOTES

Chapter 5

Shyness Isn't the Issue; Fear Is

Separating temperament from trauma

SYMPTOM

"This is just how I've always been."

This symptom often presents as resignation rather than distress. The individual has lived with shyness for so long that it feels inseparable from identity. They describe it as something inherent, unchangeable, and deeply woven into who they are. Over time, they stop questioning whether their behavior is rooted in personality or shaped by experience. Instead, they accept limitations as fact and adjust their expectations accordingly.

The belief that shyness is fixed provides emotional relief. If this is simply who I am, then there is no need to wrestle with discomfort, challenge patterns, or confront fear. Growth feels more optional than necessary. The individual may even defend their quietness when questioned, interpreting curiosity as pressure to change. This defensiveness is not rooted in pride, but in protection. Questioning the behavior feels like questioning the self.

As a result, fear becomes invisible. Rather than being recognized as a response to past experiences, fear is absorbed into identity. The individual no longer says, "I am afraid to speak," but instead says, "I am not someone who speaks." This shift is subtle but significant. When fear becomes identity, it is no longer challenged. It is accommodated.

This symptom often coexists with a strong sense of self-awareness. The individual understands their tendencies, preferences, and limits. However, this awareness becomes restrictive when it is used to justify avoidance rather than inform growth. The person may anticipate discomfort and preemptively withdraw, believing they are simply honoring who they are rather than avoiding vulnerability.

Emotionally, this symptom can feel stabilizing while quietly limiting. The individual builds a life that minimizes exposure and maximizes predictability. They choose environments, relationships, and roles that require little visibility. While this reduces anxiety in the short term, it also narrows experience. Over time, the individual may feel restless, unfulfilled, or disconnected from their potential, yet struggle to name why.

Spiritually, this symptom creates confusion. The individual may believe God designed them this way and therefore does not expect more. They may interpret calling through the lens of temperament, if obedience will never require discomfort. This belief provides comfort, but it also prevents honest examination of whether fear has shaped what feels "natural."

TEACHING

Fear Can Shape Personality Without Being Your Personality

Scripture affirms that God forms individuals with unique temperaments, strengths, and dispositions. Personality is real, intentional, and valuable. However, Scripture also reveals that fear can influence behavior without defining identity. Throughout the Bible, people act out of fear in ways that do not reflect who God created them to be. These behaviors are addressed not by changing personality, but by restoring trust.

Fear often develops as response to experience. Pain, rejection, misunderstanding, and disappointment teach the nervous system how to stay safe. Over time, these protective responses can become habitual, shaping how a person engages with the world. When fear persists unexamined, it can masquerade as preference. What once served as protection becomes limitation.

The danger lies not in being shy, but in allowing fear to set the boundaries of obedience. God never asks individuals to abandon their temperament, but He does invite them to trust Him beyond it. When fear dictates behavior, obedience becomes selective. The individual follows God where it feels safe and hesitates where vulnerability is required.

Scripture repeatedly demonstrates that God works within temperament while challenging fear. Moses remained thoughtful and cautious, yet he still spoke when called. Jeremiah remained sensitive, yet he still proclaimed truth. These examples illustrate that personality is not an obstacle; fear is. God does not erase who a person is, but He does heal what has restricted them.

Healing begins when the individual learns to separate identity from adaptation. Recognizing fear as a response rather than a trait allows space for compassion and growth. The question shifts from "Why am I like this?" to "What taught me to live this way?" This shift removes shame and invites understanding.

God's invitation is not to become someone else, but to become freer within who you already are. When fear is identified and addressed, personality expands rather than disappears. The individual remains thoughtful, reflective, and reserved, but no longer confined by avoidance. Trust replaces self-protection, and obedience becomes less negotiated.

FAITH PRESCRIPTION

Name Fear Without Attaching It to Identity

The prescribed treatment for this diagnosis is intentional separation of fear from self-concept. The patient is encouraged to identify moments where fear influences behavior and name it accurately rather than absorbing it into identity. This practice involves replacing statements such as "This is just who I am" with "This is how I learned to protect myself."

This prescription requires patience and honesty. Fear may resist being named because it has provided a sense of safety. However, when fear is acknowledged without judgment, it loses its authority. Over time, this practice restores agency and allows personality to exist without limitation.

🧬 SPIRITUAL VITAMIN

Vitamin I: Identity
Scripture Reference: 2 Timothy 1:7

This vitamin supports clarity between who the individual is and what fear has shaped. The patient is encouraged to take this vitamin daily by affirming identity rooted in God's design rather than learned avoidance. Continued intake strengthens confidence grounded in truth rather than protection.

🕊 HOLY SPIRIT CONSULT

Holy Spirit shows me where fear has blended into my sense of self. Help me recognize what truly my personality is and what developed as protection. Teach me how to trust You with the parts of me that feel fragile or hesitant. Restore freedom where fear has set limits.

🙏 GUIDED PRAYER

"God, I thank You for the way You created me. I acknowledge that fear has influenced how I show up in the world, sometimes in ways I have mistaken for identity. Help me separate who I am from what I learned to survive.

Teach me how to trust You beyond my comfort and allow healing to reshape my responses. I choose to believe that growth does not require becoming someone else but becoming freer. Amen."

📝 JOURNAL REFLECTION PAGE

- What behaviors have I labeled as "just who I am" without examining their origins?

____

____

____

____

____

- What experiences may have taught me to associate visibility with danger?

____

____

____

____

- How might my life look different if fear no longer defined my limits?

____

____

____

- What aspects of my personality might expand if trust replaced self-protection?

PERSONAL NOTES

Chapter 6

When Humility Becomes Self-Erasure

Why Shrinking Yourself Is Not The Same As Honoring God

SYMPTOM

"I don't want to make it about me."

This symptom often feels spiritually commendable, which makes it especially difficult to recognize as harmful. The individual genuinely desires to honor God and avoid pride, arrogance, or self-promotion. They are sensitive to the dangers of ego and sincerely want their life to point toward something greater than themselves. As a result, they intentionally minimize their presence, contributions, and voice, believing that humility requires remaining small and unseen.

Over time, however, this posture begins to distort the meaning of humility. Instead of humility being an accurate view of self in relation to God, it becomes a habit of self-erasure. The individual stops offering ideas, refrains from stepping into roles where they might be noticed and consistently deflects opportunities that require visibility. These choices are not framed as fear, but as virtue. The person tells themselves  they are honoring God by staying out of the spotlight, even when the spotlight was not the goal to begin with.

As this pattern develops, the individual becomes uncomfortable with acknowledgment of any kind. Compliments are dismissed, affirmation is deflected, and responsibility is avoided under the guise of humility. The individual may believe that allowing themselves to be seen, affirmed, or trusted is spiritually dangerous. This belief gradually teaches them to disconnect from their own gifts, strengths, and calling.

Emotionally, this symptom often produces quiet resentment and confusion. The individual may feel overlooked or underutilized while simultaneously rejecting opportunities for involvement. They may desire to be valued while refusing visibility. This internal contradiction creates tension that is difficult to name because it feels inappropriate to admit frustration when one believes they are choosing humility.

Spiritually, self-erasure limits growth. God's work in a person's life often involves development, refinement, and responsibility. When humility is misunderstood as disappearance, obedience becomes selective. The individual may serve faithfully in private while resisting roles that require leadership or influence. Over time, this reinforces the belief that their presence is unnecessary or expendable.

This symptom is frequently reinforced by environments where humility is praised without clarity. Messages about dying to self or decreasing so God can increase are interpreted as invitations to vanish rather than mature. The individual internalizes the idea that taking up space is inherently prideful, even when it is an expression of stewardship and obedience.

TEACHING

Biblical Humility Requires Honesty, Not Disappearance

Scripture defines humility not as self-neglect, but as alignment with truth. Humility involves recognizing dependence on God while also acknowledging the gifts, responsibilities, and identity He has given. Jesus modeled humility through obedience and service, not through invisibility. He withdrew, when necessary, but He did not erase Himself. He taught openly, led confidently, and accepted responsibility for His role.

Biblical humility does not deny value; it places value in proper context. When individuals erase themselves in the name of humility, they misrepresent God's design. God does not ask His people to disappear; He asks them to serve faithfully with integrity. Self-erasure contradicts stewardship, because it withholds what God has entrusted.

Scripture consistently shows God elevating individuals into responsibility rather than hiding them indefinitely. Joseph was raised into leadership. Deborah judged openly. Esther was positioned visibly. These examples demonstrate that humility and visibility are not opposite. Obedience often requires presence, accountability, and influence.

When humility becomes self-erasure, fear often plays a hidden role. Fear of pride, fear of criticism, and fear of responsibility can masquerade as reverence. The individual may believe they are 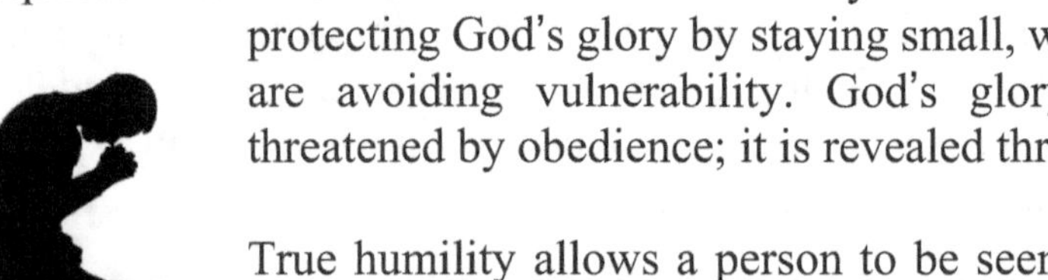 protecting God's glory by staying small, when they are avoiding vulnerability. God's glory is not threatened by obedience; it is revealed through it.

True humility allows a person to be seen without self-promotion and to accept responsibility without self-exaltation. It involves offering one's gifts freely, trusting God to guard the heart against pride. Humility does not require silence when God invites speech, nor absence when God invites leadership.

Healing begins when humility is reframed as honesty rather than disappearance. The individual learns that acknowledging gifts does not negate dependence on God. Instead, it honors the One who gave them. When fear is removed from humility, obedience becomes clearer and less burdened by self-doubt.

💊 FAITH PRESCRIPTION

Practice Humility Without Hiding

The prescribed treatment for self-erasure is intentional participation rooted in obedience rather than self-evaluation. The patient is encouraged to accept responsibility, speak when prompted, and contribute openly without attaching worth to visibility. This practice retrains humility as stewardship rather than withdrawal.

 The patient should resist the impulse to disappear when noticed and instead remain present without self-promotion. Over time, this restores balance between dependence and responsibility, allowing humility to function as truth rather than fear.

⚕ SPIRITUAL VITAMIN

Vitamin H: Honesty
Scripture Reference: Romans 12:3

This vitamin supports accurate self-perception rooted in God's design. The patient is encouraged to take this vitamin daily by acknowledging both dependence on God and responsibility to steward what has been given. Continued intake strengthens humility that is grounded in truth rather than fear.

🕊 HOLY SPIRIT CONSULT

Holy Spirit, show me where I have confused humility with self-erasure. Reveal the ways I have withdrawn when You were inviting me to participate. Teach me how to honor You honestly with my presence, my gifts, and my obedience without fear of pride or exposure.

🙏 GUIDED PRAYER

"God, I desire to honor You with humility, not fear. I confess that I

have hidden parts of myself believing it was virtuous. Help me understand humility as truth rather than disappearance. Teach me to accept responsibility, visibility, and growth as acts of obedience. I trust You to guard my heart as I step forward. Amen."

📝 JOURNAL REFLECTION PAGE

- Where have I minimized my presence in the name of humility?

____

____

____

- What fears surface when I consider being seen or trusted with responsibility?

____

____

____

____

- How might my understanding of humility need to change?

____

____

____

- What gifts or opportunities have I withheld that God may be inviting me to steward?

____

____

____

Chapter 7

The Cost Of Staying Unseen

How hiding slowly limits your calling, relationships, and joy

SYMPTOM

"At least I'm not causing problems."

This symptom often develops quietly and is reinforced by positive feedback that misunderstands what is happening. The individual is rarely confrontational, seldom demanding, and generally easy to work with. They are described as agreeable, low-maintenance, and cooperative. On the surface, this appears healthy and even admirable. However, beneath this calm exterior is often a pattern of self-suppression that has gone unexamined for too long.

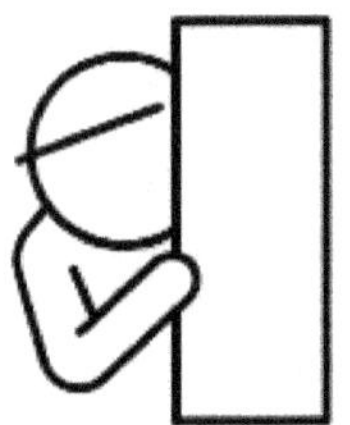

The individual avoids conflict not because they lack opinions or convictions, but because disagreement feels threatening. They minimize their needs, defer decisions, and accept outcomes they do not fully agree with to preserve peace. Over time, this habit becomes internalized as identity. The person begins to believe that staying quiet is the same as being kind and that visibility automatically creates tension or trouble.

As a result, the individual slowly disappears from meaningful participation. They attend gatherings but rarely engage deeply. They serve faithfully but avoid influence. They remain present physically while withdrawing emotionally. This form of invisibility is subtle and socially acceptable, which makes it difficult to recognize it as a problem. The individual is not overtly unhappy, but they are also not fully alive.

Emotionally, this symptom creates a growing sense of dissatisfaction. The individual may feel overlooked or undervalued, yet also responsible for maintaining harmony. They may suppress frustration, disappointment, or grief because expressing these emotions feels disruptive. Over time, this emotional suppression leads to numbness or quiet resentment, even toward situations they chose to remain silent about.

Relationally, staying unseen limits connection. Relationships remain polite but shallow. Others may appreciate the individual's flexibility without truly knowing them. Because needs and boundaries are rarely expressed, misunderstandings accumulate. The individual may feel lonely even when surrounded by people, unsure why connection feels elusive.

Spiritually, this symptom restricts growth. Calling often involves responsibility, influence, and visibility. When an individual consistently avoids these elements, their sense of purpose diminishes. They may feel stuck, wondering why life feels smaller than expected. This stagnation is not due to lack of faith, but to the habit of remaining unseen.

TEACHING

Peacekeeping Is Not The Same As Peacemaking

Scripture distinguishes between avoiding conflict and pursuing peace. True peace is not achieved by erasing oneself or suppressing truth. Jesus consistently modeled peacemaking through honesty, presence, and courage. He did not avoid tension when truth was required, nor did He seek harmony at the expense of integrity. 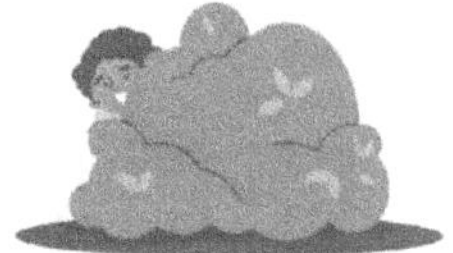

Peacemaking involves engagement, not disappearance. It requires clarity, communication, and willingness to be known. When individuals stay unseen to avoid discomfort, they may preserve surface-level calm, but they sacrifice authenticity. Over time, this approach limits relational depth and emotional health.

Jesus taught that His followers are called to be salt and light, both of which require presence. Salt that remains unused has no impact. Light that is hidden provides no guidance. These metaphors

emphasize that faith and calling are meant to interact with the world, not retreat from it.

Avoiding visibility may feel protective, but it also limits joy. Joy is often found in meaningful contribution, honest connection, and shared purpose. When individuals hide, they miss opportunities to experience fulfillment that comes from being fully engaged. God's design for joy includes participation, not withdrawal.

Peacemaking sometimes requires uncomfortable conversations, expressed boundaries, and visible leadership. These actions may introduce tension in the short term, but they ultimately produce growth and understanding. When fear prevents engagement, peace becomes fragile and dependent on silence rather than truth.

Healing begins when individuals recognize that staying unseen carries a cost. Avoidance may reduce immediate stress, but it slowly erodes purpose, connection, and joy. God's invitation is not to live problem-free, but to live fully. Presence, even when imperfect, creates space for authentic peace.

℘ FAITH PRESCRIPTION

Practice Presence Even When It Feels Risky

The prescribed treatment for the cost of staying unseen is intentional engagement. The patient is encouraged to express thoughts, needs, and boundaries respectfully and honestly. This practice may feel disruptive at first, but it restores balance between peace and truth.

The patient should begin with low-risk situations and gradually increase engagement as confidence grows. Over time, presence becomes less threatening, and relationships deepen. Fear loses its influence as the individual experience's connection without self-erasure.

⚕ SPIRITUAL VITAMIN

Vitamin C: Courage

Scripture Reference: Joshua 1:9

This vitamin supports emotional and spiritual strength when engagement feels intimidating. The patient is encouraged to take this vitamin daily by choosing honesty over avoidance. Continued intake builds courage rooted in trust rather than control.

🕊 HOLY SPIRIT CONSULT

Holy Spirit shows me where staying unseen has cost me connection, purpose, or joy. Help me recognize when I have chosen silence to avoid discomfort rather than pursue peace. Teach me how to engage honestly and trust You with the outcomes of presence.

🙏 GUIDED PRAYER

God, I acknowledge that staying unseen has felt safer than stepping forward. I confess that I have avoided engagement to prevent tension and discomfort. Teach me how to pursue peace through honesty and presence rather than silence. Help me trust You with my relationships, my calling, and my joy as I choose to be fully present. Amen.

📝 JOURNAL REFLECTION PAGE

- Where have I stayed silent to avoid conflict or discomfort?

____

____

____

____

____

____

____

- How has staying unseen affected my relationships and sense of purpose?

____

____

____

____

____

- What emotions have I suppressed to maintain peace?

____

____

____

____

____

- What is one area where God may be inviting me to step into greater presence?

____

____

____

____

Part 3:

THE TREATMENT PLAN

Healing without becoming someone else

PERSONAL NOTES

Chapter 8

Courage Without Volume

Learning to show up without performing confidence

SYMPTOM

"I'm just not bold like other people."

This symptom is often shaped by comparison rather than conviction. The individual measures themselves against louder, more expressive personalities and concludes that courage must look a certain way. Because they do not match that image, they assume they lack courage altogether. This belief creates unnecessary pressure to perform confidence rather than practice presence, leading many to withdraw instead of engaging.

The individual may associate courage with extroversion, quick responses, and visible assertiveness. When they cannot meet those expectations, they interpret their discomfort as inadequacy. This misunderstanding reinforces the belief that showing up requires becoming someone else. Over time, the individual may stop attempting to engage because they feel they will never measure up to the perceived standard of boldness.

Emotionally, this symptom produces self-criticism and discouragement. The individual may admire courage in others while doubting their own capacity for it. They may overlook the quiet ways they already demonstrate courage, such as consistency, thoughtfulness, or endurance. Because these qualities are less visible, they are undervalued.

Spiritually, this symptom limits obedience. The individual may hesitate to act when obedience does not align with their understanding of courage. They wait for a feeling of boldness that never arrives, believing courage should precede action rather than result from it. This delay reinforces fear and diminishes trust in God's ability to work through quiet strength.

TEACHING

Biblical Courage Is Faithful Presence, Not Personality

Scripture presents courage in many forms, not all of them loud or confrontational. Courage often appears as obedience in the face of fear, not the absence of it. Many biblical figures acted courageously while still experiencing hesitation, doubt, or discomfort. Their courage was rooted in trust rather than temperament.

God does not require a specific personality type to demonstrate courage. He calls individuals to act faithfully within who they are. Courage emerges when trust overrides fear, even briefly. It is not a performance to be perfected, but a practice to be developed.

When individuals equate courage with volume, they miss opportunities to act in ways that align with their design. Courage may look like staying in the room, speaking one honest sentence, or accepting responsibility without fanfare. These acts, though quiet, are no less powerful.

Faith grows when courage is practiced consistently rather than dramatically. God honors obedience that is sincere, even when it is understated. Courage without volume allows individuals to show up authentically without performing confidence.

FAITH PRESCRIPTION

Practice Courage That Fits Who You Are

The prescribed treatment for this symptom is redefining courage as faithful presence rather than outward boldness. The patient is encouraged to act within their capacity while gently stretching beyond comfort. This involves choosing obedience without demanding emotional certainty or performative confidence.

Over time, consistent action builds trust and diminishes fear. Courage becomes less intimidating as it is practiced in manageable ways. The patient learns that courage does not require becoming someone else but trusting God within who they already are.

SPIRITUAL VITAMIN

Vitamin F: Faithfulness
Scripture Reference: Luke 16:10

This vitamin supports steady obedience and quiet courage. The patient is encouraged to take this vitamin daily by honoring small acts of faithfulness. Continued intake builds confidence rooted in consistency rather than comparison.

HOLY SPIRIT CONSULT

Holy Spirit shows me where I have misunderstood courage. Help me recognize the quiet ways You invite me to show up faithfully. Teach me how to trust You with my presence without performing confidence or comparing myself to others.

GUIDED PRAYER

"God, I confess that I have believed courage required a personality I do not have. Help me redefine courage as obedience rooted in trust rather than volume.

Teach me how to show up faithfully, even when I feel uncomfortable. I trust You to work through who I am, not who I think I should be. Amen."

📝 JOURNAL REFLECTION PAGE

- Where have I compared my courage to someone else's personality?

- What quiet acts of courage have I overlooked in my own life?

- How might my understanding of courage need to change?

- What is one small step of faithful presence I can practice this week?

PERSONAL NOTES

Chapter 9

Obedience That Doesn't Require A Personality Makeover

Following God without pretending to be bold

SYMPTOM

If I were more confident, obedience would be easier."

This symptom is rooted in the belief that obedience is something reserved for people who feel naturally assertive, emotionally steady, or socially comfortable. The individual assumes that courage and confidence must come first, and that obedience will follow once those internal conditions are met. Because they do not experience themselves as naturally confident, they conclude that obedience will always feel difficult or delayed until they somehow become someone else.

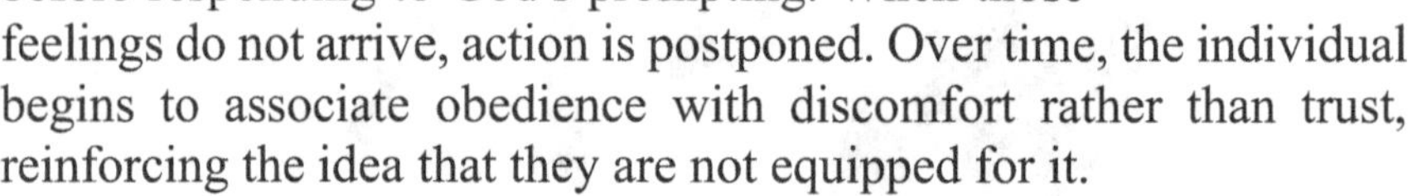

As this belief settles in, obedience becomes conditional. The individual waits for internal readiness, emotional stability, or a sense of certainty before responding to God's prompting. When those feelings do not arrive, action is postponed. Over time, the individual begins to associate obedience with discomfort rather than trust, reinforcing the idea that they are not equipped for it.

This symptom is often reinforced by observing others who appear confident in their faith. The individual compares their internal struggle to the outward composure of others and assumes they are lacking something essential. They may admire obedience in others while quietly exempting themselves, believing that their temperament makes obedience more complicated or risky.

Emotionally, this symptom produces discouragement and self-doubt. The individual may want to follow God fully but feel limited by their perceived shortcomings. They may believe that obedience requires a stronger personality, thicker skin, or greater emotional resilience than they possess. This belief gradually undermines trust in God's ability to work through weakness.

Spiritually, this symptom leads to passivity. The individual continues to believe and desire obedience, but action remains inconsistent. Over time, the gap between intention and action grows wider, creating frustration and spiritual fatigue. The individual may question why faith feels sincere but progress feels slow.

TEACHING

God Never Required Confidence Before Obedience

Scripture consistently demonstrates that obedience often precedes confidence rather than results from it. Many biblical figures acted while still unsure, fearful, or reluctant. Moses obeyed despite insecurity. Peter followed despite impulsiveness and doubt. The disciples acted before fully understanding Jesus 'mission. These examples reveal that God does not wait for emotional readiness before calling people to act.

Obedience is an act of trust, not self-assurance. It does not require a personality overhaul or emotional certainty. It requires willingness. When individuals wait for confidence before obeying, they invert the relationship between trust and action. Confidence grows through obedience, not the other way around.

God works through personality rather than against it. He does not ask individuals to abandon who they are, but He does invite them to trust Him beyond their comfort. Obedience that aligns with temperament allows individuals to act faithfully without performing confidently. Quiet obedience is no less valid than visible obedience. When obedience is practiced imperfectly, faith deepens. Each act of obedience reinforces trust and reduces fear. Over time, confidence emerges naturally, rooted in experience rather than imagination. God's power is revealed not through self-assurance, but through dependence.

Healing occurs when individuals stop waiting to feel ready and start responding in trust. Obedience becomes less intimidating when it is viewed as partnership rather than performance. God honors faith expressed through willingness, even when confidence is absent.

FAITH PRESCRIPTION

Respond in Trust, Not Confidence

The prescribed treatment for conditional obedience is practicing response without requiring emotional certainty. The patient is encouraged to act when clarity is present, even if confidence is not. This practice shifts the focus from internal readiness to relational trust.

Over time, consistent response builds familiarity with obedience. Fear diminishes as experience replaces imagination. The patient learns that obedience does not demand confidence, but trust in God's presence throughout the process.

SPIRITUAL VITAMIN

Vitamin O: Obedience
Scripture Reference: John 14:15

This vitamin strengthens the connection between love and action. The patient is encouraged to take this vitamin daily by responding to God's prompting in small, manageable ways. Continued intake builds faith rooted in trust rather than emotional readiness.

HOLY SPIRIT CONSULT

Holy Spirit shows me where I have delayed obedience because I believed confidence was required first. Help me trust You enough to respond even when I feel uncertain. Teach me how to obey without performing and how to grow through experience rather than waiting for readiness.

🙏 GUIDED PRAYER

"God, I acknowledge that I have waited to feel confident before obeying You. I confess that this has delayed growth and limited trust. Teach me how to respond in faith rather than certainty.

Help me trust You with my weakness and believe that obedience itself will shape confidence. I choose to follow You as I am, not as I think I should be. Amen."

📝 JOURNAL REFLECTION PAGE

- Where have I waited for confidence before responding to God?

____

____

____

____

____

- How has this belief affected my willingness to obey?

____

____

____

____

____

- What might change if I viewed obedience as trust rather than performance?

____

____

____

____

- What is one area where I can respond in obedience without waiting to feel ready?

____

Chapter 10

Being Seen Without Losing Yourself

How to step forward without betraying who you are

SYMPTOM

"If I let people see me, I'll lose myself."

This symptom is rooted in the belief that visibility requires compromise. The individual fears that being seen will force them to become someone they are not, adopt expectations they cannot sustain, or abandon boundaries that protect their emotional and spiritual well-being. As a result, visibility is associated with loss rather than growth. Remaining unseen feels like the only way to preserve authenticity and control.

People experiencing this symptom often have a strong sense of self internally. They know what they value, what drains them, and what matters to them. However, they also carry memories of situations where being visible led to pressure, misinterpretation, or demands they were not prepared to meet. These experiences teach them that exposure comes at the cost of selfhood. Over time, the safest way to remain whole seems to be staying hidden.

This belief creates hesitation around leadership, influence, or deeper engagement. The individual may fear being labeled, boxed in, or misunderstood once they step forward. They worry that others will project expectations onto them that do not align with who they truly are. As a result, they limit their presence to avoid the risk of being defined by others.

Emotionally, this symptom produces guardedness. The individual carefully manages how much of themselves are visible, revealing only what feels safe. While this strategy preserves control, it also restricts connection. The individual may feel known by God but unknown by people, which reinforces isolation. Over time, this guardedness can feel exhausting, requiring constant self-monitoring.

Spiritually, this symptom leads to tension between calling and protection. The individual senses invite greater responsibility or influence but resist them out of fear of losing authenticity. They may believe that staying hidden preserves integrity, while stepping forward invites compromise. This belief keeps obedience limited and reinforces the idea that faith and selfhood are at odds.

TEACHING

God Does Not Reveal You in Order to Erase You

Scripture consistently affirms that God's work in a person's life restores identity rather than diminishes it. Being seen by God is not an act of exposure meant to strip away authenticity, but an act of affirmation that brings wholeness. God calls individuals forward not to reshape them into something artificial, but to refine what He has already created.

Throughout Scripture, God reveals people gradually and intentionally. He does not overwhelm individuals with visibility or responsibility without preparation. Jesus invited His disciples into increasing levels of exposure, authority, and accountability over time. This process allowed them to grow without losing themselves. Visibility was not forced; it was formed.

The fear of losing oneself often stems from confusing visibility with people-pleasing. When individuals believe that being seen requires meeting everyone's expectations, visibility feels threatening. However, obedience to God does not require conformity to others' demands. God calls people to faithfulness, not performance. Being seen in obedience allows identity to strengthen rather than dissolve. God's invitation to visibility includes boundaries. Scripture models seasons of engagement and withdrawal, leadership and rest. Jesus Himself withdrew to pray and rest, demonstrating that visibility does not eliminate the need for limits. Authentic presence involves discernment, not self-abandonment.

Healing occurs when individuals trust that God can protect their identity as they step forward. Visibility does not require surrendering values, personality, or boundaries. It requires trusting God to anchor identity while expanding influence. When fear no longer equates visibility with loss, obedience becomes less threatening and more life-giving.

🔖 FAITH PRESCRIPTION

Practice Visible Obedience While Maintaining Boundaries

The prescribed treatment for this symptom is intentional visibility paired with clear boundaries. The patient is encouraged to engage in opportunities for presence while remaining attentive to personal limits. This practice reinforces the truth that being seen does not require self-erasure or overextension.

The patient should communicate needs honestly, decline roles that exceed capacity, and trust God to guide exposure. Over time, this balanced approach restores confidence and reduces fear. Visibility becomes an expression of obedience rather than a threat to identity.

🧬 SPIRITUAL VITAMIN

Vitamin B — Boundaries
Scripture Reference: Mark 1:35

This vitamin supports sustainable presence and authentic engagement. The patient is encouraged to take this vitamin daily by honoring limits and seeking renewal. Continued intake strengthens identity rooted in God's design rather than external expectations.

🕊 HOLY SPIRIT CONSULT

Holy Spirit shows me where I have equated being seen with losing myself. Help me trust You to protect my identity as I step forward. Teach me how to engage with boundaries, clarity, and authenticity. Guide me into visibility that aligns with who You created me to be.

🙏 GUIDED PRAYER

"God, I confess that I have feared being seen because I believed it would cost me my sense of self. I thank You for creating me with intention and care.

Teach me how to trust You with my visibility and my boundaries. Help me step forward in obedience without compromising who I am. I choose to believe that You reveal me to restore me, not erase me. Amen."

📝 JOURNAL REFLECTION PAGE

- What fears surface when I consider being more visible?

____

____

____

____

- Where have I equated obedience with self-loss?

____

____

____

____

____

____

- What boundaries do I need to maintain as I step forward?

____

____

____

____

- How might my identity strengthen if I trusted God with my visibility?

____

____

____

____

____

____

____

Part 4:

AFTERCARE
Staying present when hiding feels easier

PERSONAL NOTES

Chapter 11

When Fear Tries To Take The Mic Back

Why doesn't progress mean fear disappears

SYMPTOM

"I thought I was past this."

This symptom often appears after meaningful growth has already taken place. The individual has taken steps toward visibility, practiced obedience, and experienced moments of courage that once felt impossible. Because of this progress, the return of fear feels confusing and discouraging. The individual may believe that fear's reappearance means something has gone wrong or that earlier growth was not genuine.

Fear rarely leaves permanently after initial healing. Instead, it resurfaces in familiar situations, often triggered by stress, fatigue, or new levels of responsibility. The individual notices old thoughts returning, such as questioning whether it is safer to stay quiet or wondering if stepping forward was a mistake. These thoughts do not necessarily erase progress, but they challenge it. The individual may feel tempted to retreat, believing that withdrawal will restore emotional balance.

Emotionally, this symptom produces disappointment and self-criticism. The individual may judge themselves harshly for feeling afraid again, interpreting fear as failure rather than a signal. This judgment intensifies anxiety and creates pressure to maintain growth perfectly. Instead of recognizing fear as a normal response to change, the individual internalizes it as a personal flaw.

Behaviorally, fear's return may lead to subtle withdrawal. The individual might reduce engagement, delay responses, or minimize presence without fully realizing it. These small retreats can feel justified as self-care or caution, but over time they reestablish old patterns. The individual may feel torn between the desire to protect progress and the instinct to avoid discomfort.

Spiritually, this symptom creates confusion about trust. The individual may wonder why faith feels harder again or why courage feels inconsistent. They may question whether growth was temporary or whether fear will always have the final word. This uncertainty can undermine confidence and lead to discouragement if not addressed honestly.

TEACHING

Fear's Return Is Not Failure, It Is A Signal

Scripture consistently portrays growth as a process rather than a straight line. Many biblical figures experienced recurring fear even after moments of courage. David trusted God deeply yet still wrestled with anxiety. Elijah demonstrated bold faith and later fled in fear. These examples show that fear's return does not negate growth; it reveals areas that are still being strengthened.

Fear often reappears when responsibility increases or when visibility expands. This does not mean the individual has regressed. It means new ground is being covered. Growth exposes deeper layers of fear that were previously hidden, not because healing failed, but because capacity increased. Fear surfaces to be addressed at a new level.

Aftercare is essential because progress requires maintenance. Just as physical healing requires follow-up care, emotional and spiritual growth require attention. Without aftercare, old patterns may quietly reassert themselves. With intentional awareness, however, fear loses its authority more quickly each time it appears.

God does not expect fearless consistency. He invites honest persistence. Trust is not measured by the absence of fear, but by response to it. When individuals recognize fear as a cue rather than a command, they remain present instead of retreating. This distinction transforms fear from a threat into an opportunity for continued growth.

Fear's voice often sounds familiar, but familiarity does not equal truth. The individual learns to notice fear without obeying it. Over time, fear's influence diminishes as trust becomes more practiced. Growth stabilizes when the individual understands that courage is sustained through repetition rather than perfection.

💊 FAITH PRESCRIPTION

Respond to Fear Without Retreating

The prescribed treatment for fear's return is intentional engagement rather than avoidance. The patient is encouraged to remain present in situations that trigger old fears, while practicing previously learned responses. This does not require forcing confidence but choosing not to withdraw.

The patient should acknowledge fear without judgment and continue engaging at a manageable pace. Over time, repeated exposure without retreat retrains emotional responses and reinforces trust. Fear loses strength when it is faced consistently rather than avoided.

SPIRITUAL VITAMIN

Vitamin P: Perseverance
Scripture Reference: Galatians 6:9

This vitamin supports sustained growth and resilience. The patient is encouraged to take this vitamin daily by continuing faithful actions even when fear resurfaces. Continued intake strengthens endurance rooted in trust rather than emotion.

HOLY SPIRIT CONSULT

Holy Spirit, help me to recognize fear without believing it defines my progress. Show me how to remain present when old patterns resurface. Teach me how to respond with trust rather than retreat. Strengthen me to persevere through discomfort and continue growing.

🙏 GUIDED PRAYER

"God, I confess that when fear returns, I often assume I have failed. Help me see fear as a signal rather than a verdict. Teach me how to stay present and trust You even when discomfort resurfaces.

I choose perseverance over retreat and trust You to complete the work You have begun in me. Amen."

📝 JOURNAL REFLECTION PAGE

- When fear resurfaces, what thoughts immediately follow?

____

____

____

____

____

- How do I typically respond to fear after making progress?

____

____

____

____

____

- What has helped me remain present in the past?

____

____

____

____

____

- How might perseverance look different from perfection in my life?

____

____

____

____

____

____

____

____

____

____

____

Chapter 12

Practicing Presence In A World That Rewards Loudness

Staying grounded when visibility is measured by volume

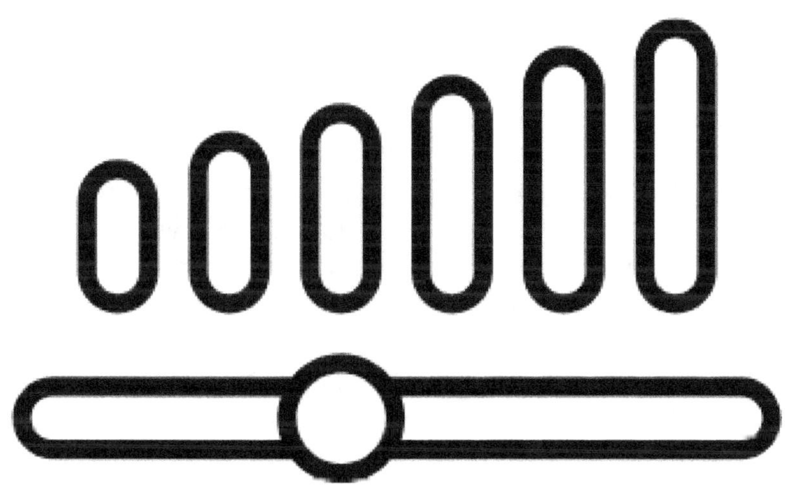

SYMPTOM

"I just don't fit in a world like this."

This symptom often develops in response to cultural environments that prioritize visibility, speed, and assertiveness. The individual observes that those who speak quickly, promote themselves confidently, and command attention are often rewarded with influence and opportunity. In contrast, those who are reflective, reserved, or measured may feel overlooked. Over time, this contrast leads the individual to believe that their way of being is incompatible with success, leadership, or impact.

The individual may internalize the message that presence must be loud to be effective. Because they do not naturally operate this way, they begin to feel out of place. They may question whether their contributions matter or whether their temperament is a disadvantage that must be overcome. This belief reinforces withdrawal and self-doubt, making presence feel like a constant uphill effort.

Emotionally, this symptom produces fatigue and discouragement. The individual expends energy comparing themselves to louder personalities and measuring their worth against external standards. This comparison diminishes confidence and creates pressure to perform in ways that feel unnatural. Over time, the individual may disengage altogether, believing that participation is futile in environments that do not value their strengths.

Spiritually, this symptom can distort calling. The individual may assume that God's work aligns with cultural expectations of boldness and visibility. They may believe that impact requires adopting behaviors that conflict with their design. This assumption leads to tension between faith and identity, where obedience feels like assimilation rather than authenticity.

TEACHING

God's Measure of Presence Is Faithfulness, Not Volume

Scripture consistently challenges cultural definitions of influence and success. God often works through those who are overlooked rather than celebrated. Biblical impact is not measured by visibility, but by obedience. Many of God's most effective servants operated quietly, faithfully, and persistently, without public recognition.

The world may reward loudness, but God honors faithfulness. Presence, in God's economy, is about availability rather than attention. It involves showing up consistently, listening attentively, and responding obediently. These qualities are not diminished by quietness; they are often strengthened by it.

Jesus modeled presence that was both visible and grounded. He engaged crowds, but He also withdrew. He taught publicly, yet valued solitude. His life demonstrates that presence is not constant exposure, but intentional engagement aligned with purpose. This balance offers a framework for practicing presence without sacrificing identity.

When individuals attempt to match cultural expectations of loudness, they often experience burnout and disconnection. Authentic presence requires alignment between inner life and outward action. God invites individuals to participate in His work without abandoning who they are. Faithfulness expressed through quiet consistency carries enduring impact.

Practicing presence in a loud world requires discernment. The individual learns to engage meaningfully without competing for attention. They recognize that their contributions matter even when they are not the most noticeable. Over time, this understanding restores confidence and allows presence to become sustainable rather than performative.

⬭ FAITH PRESCRIPTION

Engage Consistently Without Competing

The prescribed treatment for this symptom is intentional engagement rooted in faithfulness rather than comparison. The patient is encouraged to show up regularly, contribute thoughtfully, and remain grounded in purpose. This practice reinforces the truth that presence does not require constant visibility.

The patient should release the need to be noticed and focus instead on being available. Over time, consistent engagement builds trust and influence organically. Loudness becomes unnecessary when faithfulness is practiced.

SPIRITUAL VITAMIN

Vitamin G: Groundedness
Scripture Reference: Colossians 2:6–7

This vitamin supports stability and confidence rooted in Christ rather than cultural standards. The patient is encouraged to take this vitamin daily by remaining anchored in identity and purpose. Continued intake strengthens resilience and reduces comparison.

HOLY SPIRIT CONSULT

Holy Spirit, help me practice presence without competing for attention. Teach me how to remain grounded in who You created me to be. Show me where comparison has diminished my confidence and guided me toward faithful engagement that aligns with Your purposes.

🙏 GUIDED PRAYER

"God, I confess that I have compared myself to louder voices and questioned my place in the world. Help me trust that You value faithfulness over visibility.

Teach me how to show up consistently without performing or competing. I choose to remain grounded in You as I practice presence in a world that rewards loudness. Amen."

📝 JOURNAL REFLECTION PAGE

- Where do I feel pressure to be louder or more visible than feel authentic?

____

____

____

____

____

- How has comparison affected my willingness to engage?

____

____

____

____

____

- What does faithful presence look like for me in my current season?

____

- How can I remain grounded while participating meaningfully in a loud world?

Epilogue

This Is Me

If you have made it to this point, something in you has already changed, even if you cannot fully name it yet. People often expect conclusions to offer relief, resolution, or a sense of arrival, but healing rarely works that way. What you are experiencing now is not completion, but clarity.

You are no longer guessing why you have felt stuck, invisible, hesitant, or conflicted. You now understand that what looked like personality alone was often protection layered over fear, shaped by experience, reinforced by misunderstanding, and quietly baptized as virtue.

This matters, because clarity is what allows choice.

For much of your life, you did not choose to hide. You adapted. You learned what felt safe. You discovered which versions of yourself were welcomed and which were questioned, misunderstood, or ignored. Over time, those lessons shaped your behavior so subtly that you stopped noticing the cost.

You did not wake up one day and decide to shrink. You learned how to do it gradually, intelligently, and convincingly. You learned how to survive environments that reward loudness by becoming careful. You learned how to stay faithful without being vulnerable. You learned how to call silence wisdom and delay patience because it allowed you to function without confrontation.

None of that makes you weak. It makes you human. But survival is not the same as living, and protection is not the same as trust. Somewhere along the way, the strategies that kept you safe began limiting the life you were meant to live.

They did not announce themselves as barriers. They felt responsible, spiritual, and reasonable. That is why they were so effective. Fear rarely shows up as panic in people like you. It shows up as overthinking, restraint, humility, and postponement. It speaks softly. It sounds logical. It blends into your identity until you stop questioning whether it belongs there.

This book was never about turning you into someone louder, bolder, or more socially impressive. It was about giving you permission to stop mistaking fear for faithfulness and silence for obedience. It was about helping you see that God has never been disappointed in your quiet, but He has always been invested in your presence. He has not been waiting for you to change your personality. He has been waiting for you to stop disappearing inside it.

What makes this moment different is that you can no longer claim ignorance. You know now when you are hiding. You recognize the language fear uses with you. You can tell the difference between waiting and avoiding, between humility and self-erasure, between peace and disengagement. This does not mean you will always choose perfectly. It means you will choose consciously.

And that changes everything.

From here on, your growth will not look dramatic. It will look consistent. It will not feel loud. It will feel honest. You will still have days when speaking feels difficult, when presence feels costly, and when retreating seems tempting. The difference is that you will no longer confuse those feelings with instruction. Fear will still speak, but it will no longer sound authoritative. It will sound familiar, and familiarity is no longer convincing.

You will notice something subtle but powerful as you practice presence without performance. Your life will start to feel larger, not because you are doing more, but because you are no longer shrinking. Conversations will deepen. Relationships will feel more mutual. Faith will feel less theoretical and more embodied. Obedience will stop feeling like a threat to your identity and start feeling like a partnership with God.

You will also discover that being seen does not cost you the way you once feared. In fact, the opposite will happen. The more honestly you show up, the more clearly you will recognize yourself. Identity strengthens through alignment, not avoidance. Each small act of presence will reinforce the truth that you are capable of more than fear allowed you to believe. Confidence will not arrive as a feeling. It will emerge as a byproduct of experience.

There will be moments when people misunderstand you. There will be situations where presence creates tension. There will be seasons when obedience feels inconvenient or uncomfortable. None of this means you are doing it wrong. It means you are participating. Life lived honestly always carries friction. The goal was never to eliminate discomfort. The goal was to stop letting discomfort decide the shape of your life.

- ✓ You were not designed to live edited.
- ✓ You were not created to be invisible to be faithful.
- ✓ You were not asked to trade authenticity for acceptance or obedience for safety.

God does not need you to compete in a world obsessed with volume. He needs you available in the life He gave you. Your contribution does not need to look like anyone else's to be valuable. It needs to be present. It needs to be honest. It needs to be lived.

As you leave this book, you may feel both grounded and unsettled, and that is normal. Growth often feels like standing on familiar ground with unfamiliar freedom.

You are still you. Your temperament remains.
Your sensitivity remains.
Your thoughtfulness remains.

What has changed is not who you are, but what you are willing to do with who you are.

- ✓ You no longer need permission to exist visibly.
- ✓ You no longer need to apologize for taking up space.
- ✓ You no longer need to wait until fear agrees.

Presence is now your practice. Trust is now your posture. Obedience is now something you step into as you are, not something you postpone until you feel different. You will learn, over time, that showing up imperfectly is far more transformative than hiding perfectly.

And when fear returns, as it will from time to time, you will not panic. You will recognize it as a signal, not a sentence. You will remember that growth is not measured by the absence of fear, but by the refusal to let fear be the final voice. You will choose presence again, not because it is easy, but because it is honest.

This is not the end of your work. It is the end of your hiding.

You are allowed to live a life that reflects your faith without betraying your nature. You are allowed to be quiet and courageous, thoughtful and obedient, reserved and present. These qualities are not contradictory. They are combinations God has always known how to use.

So go slowly if you need to but go honestly. Speak when prompted. Stay when tempted to retreat. Respond when fear says later. Let your life expand naturally as trust replaces protection. You do not owe the world a performance. You owe yourself the truth.

This is you choosing to live aligned instead of edited.
This is your practicing presence without pretending.
This is you no longer shrinking to survive.
This is you, standing fully in the life God has been inviting you into all along.
This is not a slogan.
This is not a moment.

This is a way of living. And finally, without explanation, without apology, and without fear quietly clearing its throat in the background, you are free to say it and mean it:
This is me.

FAITH CLINIC DISCHARGE PLAN

You are released, but not back into hiding

DISCHARGE SUMMARY

You are not being discharged because everything feels easy now. You are being discharged because you now understand what has been happening beneath the surface of your silence. You have learned to distinguish between personality and protection, between humility and self-erasure, and between patience and fear-based delay. You have recognized that shyness was never the enemy, but that fear quietly took advantage of it.

This discharge does not mean fear will never return. It means fear no longer has authority to define your obedience. You are leaving this clinic with clarity, not pressure. You are not expected to become louder, bolder, or more visible than who you are. You are expected to remain present, honest, and responsive to God within the life you are living.

Healing, in this case, does not look like confidence without effort. It looks like presence without hiding. It looks like obedience that fits your temperament rather than fights it. You are not being sent out to perform. You are being released to live aligned.

THE 30-DAY PRESENCE RESET

Small steps for people who learned how to disappear.

This reset is designed to retrain presence without overwhelming your nervous system or violating your personality. The goal is consistency, not intensity. Each day invites you to practice one small act of presence that gently challenges fear while honoring who you are.

During the first week, the focus is awareness. You are encouraged to notice when you feel the urge to withdraw, stay silent, or delay. Rather than correcting yourself immediately, simply observe the moment and name what is happening. Awareness is the first form of healing.

During the second week, the focus shifts to response. You are invited to choose one small act of presence each day. This may involve speaking one honest sentence, staying in a room slightly longer than you want to, or responding promptly instead of postponing. These actions should feel slightly uncomfortable but manageable.

The third week emphasizes consistency. You are encouraged to repeat acts of presence even when motivation fluctuates. This week reinforces the understanding that courage grows through repetition rather than emotional readiness.

The final week centers on integration. You reflect on how presence has changed your experience of faith, relationships, and self-perception. You begin identifying which practices you want to carry forward, recognizing that healing is sustained through ongoing awareness rather than completion.

DAILY SPIRITUAL CHECK-INS

Each day, you are invited to pause and ask yourself a few grounding questions. These check-ins are not meant to be exhaustive or analytical. They are meant to keep you honest and present.

You may ask yourself where you felt the urge to hide today, what you chose instead, and how it felt afterward. You may reflect on whether fear influenced your decisions or whether trust guided your response. These questions help maintain clarity without inviting self-criticism.

📝 REFLECTION & JOURNAL SPACE

Reflection is essential for integration. You are encouraged to write honestly about moments of presence and moments of retreat without judgment.

The goal is not to track perfection, but to notice patterns. Over time, reflection helps you see growth that may otherwise go unnoticed. Journaling also provides a place to process emotions that surface as you practice presence.

Fear, relief, frustration, and pride may all appear. None of these emotions disqualify you from progress. They simply reveal where healing is still unfolding.

📜 FINAL DECLARATION: THIS IS ME

"I am no longer hiding behind silence that fear taught me to call wisdom. I am learning to show up honestly, without performing or disappearing. I trust God with my presence, my pace, and my personality. I do not need to become louder to be faithful.

I choose presence over avoidance, obedience over delay, and trust over fear. This is who I am, and I will no longer apologize for being seen."

MY FINAL WORD TO YOU

You were never meant to disappear to belong. God did not design you to be invisible, nor did He ask you to compete in a world that confuses volume with value. Your presence matters because you matter, not because you are impressive, but because you are obedient.

You are not being released back into the same patterns. You are being released with awareness, with tools, and with permission to live honestly. Healing will continue as long as you remain present. This clinic will always welcome you back for reflection, recalibration, and rest. But for now, you are released.

Go live visible enough to be faithful, and quiet enough to be true.
This is you.
This is your life.
This is you choosing not to hide.

MONTHLY PROGRESS CHART: 4 WEEKS OF PRESENCE, JOY, AND TRUTH

Tracking growth without confusing feelings with failure

This chart is not meant to measure how "good" your month was. It is meant to help you see what has been happening beneath the surface over time. Healing rarely shows up as constant happiness. More often, it shows up as increased honesty, steadier presence, and quieter joy that does not depend on how visible or comfortable you felt that day.

Happiness is often reactive. It rises and falls with circumstances, comfort, and validation. Joy, on the other hand, is more subtle. Joy tends to appear after obedience, after presence, and after truth, even when emotions feel mixed. This chart helps you look back over four weeks and recognize patterns you might miss if you only evaluate yourself day by day.

Use this chart once a week, not daily. The goal is perspective, not pressure.

HOW TO USE THIS CHART

At the end of each week, pause and reflect honestly. Do not overanalyze. Do not grade yourself. Simply notice patterns. Some weeks may feel emotionally heavy but spiritually grounded. Others may feel emotionally lighter but less aligned. Both matter. Growth is not linear, and this chart is designed to honor that reality.

MONTHLY OVERVIEW

Month: _______________________________

Season of Life (optional): _______________________________

WEEK 1 REFLECTION

This week, my overall emotional state most often felt like:

☐ Light and energized

☐ Neutral but steady

☐ Heavy but grounded

☐ Drained or overwhelmed

Happiness this week seemed to come from:
(Examples: comfort, rest, approval, quiet, avoidance, accomplishment)

____

____

____

____

Joy this week seemed to show up when:
(Examples: I spoke honestly, stayed present, obeyed despite discomfort, allowed myself to be seen)

____

____

____

____

Moments, I noticed myself wanting to hide or withdraw:

____

____

____

____

____

Moments I chose presence instead:

____

____

____

____

Looking back, this week taught me:

____

____

____

____

WEEK 2 REFLECTION

This week, my overall emotional state most often felt like:

☐ Light and energized

☐ Neutral but steady

☐ Heavy but grounded

☐ Drained or overwhelmed

Happiness this week seemed to come from:

____

____

____

____

____

Joy this week seemed to show up when:

____

____

____

____

Patterns I'm noticing compared to Week 1:
(Examples: more ease, more resistance, more awareness, more fatigue)

____

____

____

____

One way fear tried to regain control this week:

____

____

____

____

One way I stayed present anyway:

____

____

____

____

____

WEEK 3 REFLECTION

This week, my overall emotional state most often felt like:

☐ Light and energized

☐ Neutral but steady

☐ Heavy but grounded

☐ Drained or overwhelmed

Happiness this week seemed to be influenced by:

____

____

____

____

Joy this week appeared even when happiness was low by:
(Examples: obedience, honesty, alignment, peace after discomfort)

____

____

____

A moment this week where I noticed growth that didn't feel exciting:

A moment when I realized I am no longer who I was four weeks ago:

WEEK 4 REFLECTION

This week, my overall emotional state most often felt like:

☐ Light and energized
☐ Neutral but steady
☐ Heavy but grounded
☐ Drained or overwhelmed

Looking back over the month, happiness tended to rise when:

Looking back over the month, joy tended to grow when:

Ways I am showing up differently than I did at the start of this month:

Ways fear still tries to influence me (without judging myself):

____

____

4-WEEK PATTERN REVIEW

Use this space to step back and look at the month.
Over the last four weeks, I noticed that joy increases when I:

____

____

____

____

Over the last four weeks, I noticed that happiness decreases when I:

____

____

____

____

What this tells me about my growth:

____

____

____

____

What I want to carry into next month:

____

____

____

____

CLOSING REFLECTION

This month, I did not need to feel good to be good. Growth does not always make me feel happy, but it often feels more honest. If you noticed increased awareness, quicker recovery after fear, or greater willingness to stay present, those are signs of real transformation. Joy tends to settle quietly after truth, not loudly after comfort.

You are not tracking perfection. You are witnessing progress.

PERSONAL NOTES

PERSONAL NOTES

PERSONAL NOTES

134

ABOUT THE AUTHOR

Dr. Patricia Tanner was born and raised in Sanford FL. She comes from a family of three siblings. Patricia Tanner is the founder of Multhai International Realty, Multhai Asset Management Services, and Multhai Investment Group which is located in Sanford, Florida. She is a graduate of the University of Central Florida, where she received a Bachelor of Science in Business Administration and a minor in Human Resources Management.

Dr. Tanner began her career shortly thereafter as a Regional Property Manager in the apartment community. Throughout her career in property management, she has built interpersonal relationships with corporate clients. She has a successful track record of increasing company revenues over $5 million annually, through hard work, commitment, creativeness, and strategic planning.

Her experience and leadership role eventually led her to achieve a Florida Real Estate Broker license. She spent fifteen years in the Real Estate field while completing a Master of Arts in Human Resources Management from Webster University, and a Master of Public Administration from Troy University. It was in this capacity that she decided to open her own brokerage company, Multhai International Realty.

In addition, Dr. Tanner finds time in her busy schedule to participate in her own Non-For-Profit Organization, Stones 2 Homes. She remains President of her organization in which she helps people build, keep, or purchase homes in affordable communities. She is the founder of PNT Property Partners in which she buys vacant land, develops it, and constructs brand new construction homes in Sanford Florida. Her overall goal is to educate and provide resources to help people overcome financial hardships and credit disadvantage to live the American Dream through homeownership in spite of economic hardship. Through her visions she will continue to grow as an entrepreneur and is willing to share her knowledge, experience, and expertise with anyone who is willing to learn.

MORE BOOKS BY THE AUTHOR

Welcome to the Faith Clinic—where your soul doesn't need to be perfect to be healed.

You've smiled through burnout. Quoted scripture while quietly unraveling. Prayed, fasted, and still felt like your faith flatlined. If that's you, Faith Clinic: Volume I is your spiritual prescription.

Dr. Patricia S. Tanner—known as The Faith Doctor—invites you into a raw, grace-filled recovery journey for the soul. With 7 powerful doses of faith-infused wisdom, this book delivers healing where performance failed and offers truth where church hurt left a scar. Designed especially for spiritually exhausted youth and young adults, each "dose" reads like an IV drip of hope for believers secretly running on empty.

You don't need to be okay to show up. You just need to be willing. The clinic is open.

NOW AVAILABLE:
www.amazon.com

Healing was just the beginning. Now it's time to grow.

If Faith Clinic Volume I met you in crisis, Volume II meets you in recovery. Because faith isn't a one-time fix—it's a lifestyle that needs maintenance, accountability, and consistency. Welcome to your follow-up care plan.

In Faith Clinic: Volume II, Dr. Patricia S. Tanner—aka The Faith Doctor—guides you through the next level of your spiritual healing journey. From navigating church trauma and burnout to facing silence from God and rediscovering purpose, this book goes deeper than devotionals. It's not about hype—it's about habits that sustain real, lasting transformation.

With raw wisdom, relatable stories, and no-shame truths, each chapter is a spiritual check-in for believers who want to thrive—not just survive. Whether you're wrestling with doubt, craving stability, or simply ready to grow up in God, this clinic is for you.

You've detoxed. Now it's time to build. Let's get you discharge-ready.

NOW AVAILABLE:
www.amazon.com

Welcome to the Faith Clinic: Anxiety Edition — where God doesn't coddle your coping mechanisms but confronts them with surgical precision.

This book is for the ones who love Jesus but still can't sleep. For the worship leaders crying in church bathrooms. For the believers who pray in spirals, fight shame on Sundays, and secretly think, "Maybe I'm the only one who can't seem to breathe through this." You're not crazy. You're just in a fight — and this book is your spiritual triage.

Inside you'll find:
- ☑ Panic attacks in pews and the prayers that still work.
- ☑ Scriptures that talk you off the ledge.
- ☑ What to do when you feel numb and God feels quiet.
- ☑ How to walk out of shame loops, judgment spirals, and performance religion.

This isn't just encouragement. It's equipment.
Because healing isn't a moment — it's a walk.

NOW AVAILABLE:

www.amazon.com

Welcome to the Faith Clinic: Stress Edition — where we don't hand you cute verses and clichés. We hand you spiritual prescriptions for real pressure, real panic, and real prayers from tired believers holding it together by a thread.

This book is for the overwhelmed—those trusting God while juggling bills, burnout, hustle culture, and holy frustration. If you've ever whispered, "God, are You even watching this mess?" this is for you.

Inside you'll find raw, soul-hitting chapters like:

- "God, I Trust You — But These Bills Keep Coming"
- "If Rest Is Holy, Why Does It Feel Like Slacking?"
- "I'm Tired of Smiling So You Won't Worry"

This isn't fluff. It's real talk for real stress—and a reminder that you're not forgotten, you're being fortified.

The Faith Clinic is open. Breathe in & take your spiritual vitamins. Healing begins here.

NOW AVAILABLE:
www.amazon.com

This isn't just a feeling — it's a flare signal from the soul. You pray, serve, and believe in God, but something deep inside is still simmering. Welcome to the Faith Clinic: Anger Edition — where suppressed emotions meet sacred intervention.

In this volume, Dr. Patricia S. Tanner guides you through spiritual triage for:

☑ Silent rage and emotional suppression

☑ The grief–anger connection

☑ Rejection wounds from childhood to church hurt

This isn't a lecture. It's a spiritual detox. No shame. No sugar-coating. Just raw, honest healing. Whether you're snapping at loved ones or silently seething under the surface, this book meets you at the boiling point—and leads you to the breakthrough.

🩺 This is the clinic.

💧 This is your moment.

And God is ready to heal the anger behind your amen.

NOW AVAILABLE:

www.amazon.com

In this powerful installment of the Faith Clinic series, Dr. Patricia S. Tanner brings biblical insight, emotional compassion, and spiritual strength to those walking through grief. Designed as a healing chamber for the soul, each "dose" of this devotional targets a different dimension of sorrow—guiding you from pain to peace, from mourning to joy.

Inside, you'll discover:

- Daily doses of Scripture-based encouragement.
- Personal reflections and prayers for each stage of grief.
- Practical faith prescriptions to help you process loss and find purpose.

Whether you are navigating the recent loss of a loved one, confronting buried grief from the past, or supporting someone else in their sorrow, this devotional offers a gentle yet powerful roadmap to healing. Come, take your seat in the Faith Clinic—where the Great Physician is ready to restore your soul.

NOW AVAILABLE:

www.amazon.com

30 Days Of Grieving

Given By The Inspiration Of God

Healing From COVID-19

Almost a year later, it hit me... My mother was gone, and I was still stuck at the hospital. I had tried everything from crying to counseling, and even prayer. Pray they told me. Trust God they insisted. But it seemed as if nothing was working. I was hurt, dealing with my reality: my mother was not coming back.

While journeying through grief, it was under the divine 'Inspiration of God' that He placed me in a trance. While I was gaining a revelation about grief, He gave me this journal, '30 Days Of Grieving.'

NOW AVAILABLE:

www.amazon.com

The 30 Days Challenge:

I Tested POSITIVE for COVID-19

If you had 30 days to live, what would you do? If you were told that you needed to prepare for a marathon in 30 days and you were completely out of shape, what would you do first? If a family member handed you one million dollars and told you that you had to figure out how to build a house (debt free), how would you execute your plan?

I'm catching you off guard with these requests, right? Well, this is exactly what COVID-19 did when it snatched my mother's life away, wrecking my entire world. I had to battle for my mother AND my faith in 30 days flat. What a challenge!

Throughout this book, I will walk you through my brief journey with COVID-19, negative of a happy ending. I will share the diary I kept while attending to my mother, and the scriptures I read, prayed, and quoted as my shield and protection.

Take the journey with me, there is healing on the other side!

NOW AVAILABLE:

www.amazon.com

Can Salvation Get You Into Heaven? The Answer Is Yes! offers a powerful and biblically grounded exploration of God's eternal plan, revealing the heart of the Gospel and the assurance of salvation through Jesus Christ.

 Unpacking life's most vital questions—Who is God? Why were we created? What does Jesus' life mean for us?—this book brings clarity to the believer's journey and confirms that salvation, once received, is eternally secure.

Whether you're seeking understanding or affirming your faith, this inspiring guide will lead you into the confidence and joy of knowing heaven is your eternal home.

NOW AVAILABLE:

www.amazon.com

The Bench That Waited is a bold and prophetic call to action for believers who've grown comfortable in church attendance but stagnant in purpose.

With raw honesty and spiritual insight, Patricia Tanner exposes the quiet crisis of passive faith—where callings are delayed and obedience is optional.

Through Scripture, stories, and reflection, this book urges readers to rise from routine, break free from spiritual stagnation, and step boldly into their Kingdom assignment. The bench has waited long enough— will you?

NOW AVAILABLE:

www.amazon.com

What happens when the Kingdom becomes a stranger?

The Godless Climb is not a rejection of faith—it is a raw, unflinching journey through what remains when belief unravels. With brutal honesty and tender grace, this book explores the spiritual free fall that follows the loss of divine certainty, the ache of unanswered prayers, and the void left when God no longer feels near.

Written for those who have quietly slipped out of the pews and into a wilderness of doubt, grief, and inner searching, this is not a triumph story—but a survival story. A confession. A sacred wrestle. Through personal reflection and prophetic insight, the author unpacks what it means to climb without a safety net, to live without the scaffolding of religious performance, and to build a new compass in the absence of old crutches.

You haven't arrived. But you're still climbing. And that is holy.

NOW AVAILABLE:

www.amazon.com

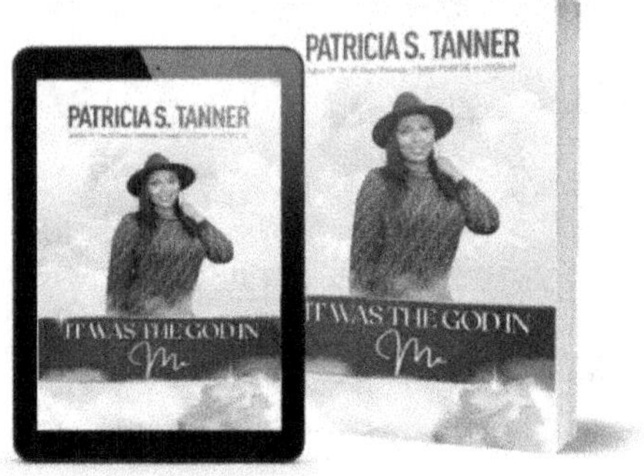

It Was The God In

Me

Success can be attributed to many things. Depending on the person who has obtained success would determine those to whom they attribute their success. Some give credit to their daily routine while others give credit to a mentor or some sort of system they followed. When I think about my success, the only person who I can give the credit to is God.

In this memoir, I share the successes and failures I have experienced throughout my life. From my individual experiences to my entrepreneurial journey, I share how God has walked with me every step of the way.

Come and see.. It Was The God In Me!!

NOW AVAILABLE:

www.amazon.com

The Triple 7 Formula is designed for business owners who are looking forward to hitting the million-dollar mark in their business. If you own a business and seem to be running in financial circles, this book will get you on track to simultaneously gaining sound business structure and millions in your bank account.

It was through many conversations with business owners lacking financial gain that prompted Patricia to share her blueprint for millionaire status. Through this book, she demonstrates how to gain financial ground by developing strong teams, implementing systems, and setting stackable goals. If you are ready to gain a laser sharp focus, and implement these clear steps, you will position yourself for financial greatness. Your business will be sound, and you will see financial growth beyond your wildest dreams!!

NOW AVAILABLE:
www.amazon.com

The Triple 7 Formula is specifically crafted for business owners aspiring to reach the million-dollar milestone. If you are a business owner feeling stuck in financial cycles, this book will set you on the path to building both a solid business structure and financial success.

This workbook is designed to complement the textbook of the same name. As you progress through its pages, you will be inspired to take decisive steps toward becoming a millionaire. From constructing your business framework to creating the millionaire's avatar, this process will expand your knowledge and mindset. Not only will you chart a course to financial success, but you will also identify your accountability circle and select a mentor to guide you toward greatness.

I cannot guarantee millionaire status unless you actively follow the steps to begin your journey. If you are searching for a get rich quick scheme, this workbook is not for you. I am looking for those ready to put in the effort—and since you are reading this, I believe that's you!

You have finally found it: Your roadmap to millions!

NOW AVAILABLE:
WWW.Amazon.com

Find Patricia on The Web:

www.PatriciaTanner.com

Follow Patricia on social media:

Facebook & Instagram: @PatriciaTannerInc